Suicide

Suicide

The Hidden Side of Modernity

CHRISTIAN BAUDELOT AND
ROGER ESTABLET

Translated by David Macey

polity

First published in French as *Suicide* © Éditions du Seuil, 2006

This English edition © Polity Press, 2008

Polity Press
65 Bridge Street
Cambridge CB2 1UR, UK

Polity Press
350 Main Street
Malden, MA 02148, USA

ISBN-13: 978-0-7456-4056-3
ISBN-13: 978-0-7456-4057-0 (pb)

A catalogue record for this book is available from the British Library.

Typeset in 11 on 13 pt Scala
by Servis Filmsetting Ltd, Stockport, Cheshire
Printed and bound in India by
Replika Press PVT Ltd, Kundli

For further information on Polity, visit our website: www.polity.co.uk

This book is supported by the French Ministry of Foreign Affairs, as part of the Burgess programme run by the Cultural Department of the French Embassy in London.
www.frenchbooknews.com

Ouvrage publié avec le concours du Ministère français chargé de la culture – Centre National du Livre.

Published with the assistance of the French Ministry of Culture – National Centre for the Book

Contents

List of figures, maps and tables DISCARD

Figures

Maps

Tables

Acknowledgements

We would like to express our profound gratitude to all those who provided us with access to data in France and other parts of the world by allowing us to consult files that have often been very under-exploited: Martine Bové (INSERM), Alain Blum, Cécile Lefevre and France Meslé (INED), Stéphanie Abrial and Daniel Masson (CIDSP, Institut de sciences politiques, Grenoble), the Commander of Police Headquarters, Pondichéry, the sociology students of the East China Normal University, Shanghai, and David Lester (Richard Stockton College of New Jersey).

We would also like to thank the staff of the various documentation centres we have consulted for the extraordinary quality of the help they gave us by broadening the horizons of our investigation: Dominique Chauvel and Maïté Ely (INED), Arlette Apkarian (Centre Asie-Pacifique, Marseille), the whole library team at the Institut d'indologie, Pondichéry and Marie-Hélène Godard (Bibliothèque Jean-Ibanès, École normale supérieure).

Jean-François Sabouret, Martine Mespoulet and Florence Bretelle helped us to arrive at a better understanding of the specific features of suicide in Japan, Russia and China. This study owes a great deal to them.

Throughout our work, we have benefited greatly from the advice and comments of our colleagues in economics and statistics: Luc Arrondel, Denis Bouget, Alexis Direr, Jérôme Gautié, Olivier Godechot, Michel Gollac and Marc Gurgand.

Drs Mocrane Abbar, Brigitte Rimlinger and their colleagues from the Fédération régionale des psychiatres du Languedoc-Roussillon provided us with the keys we needed to read the work of contemporary psychiatrists on suicide and to reach a better understanding of both the complementarity and differences between our approaches to the phenomenon.

Thanks to Pierre Surault, who gave us access to all his studies. Thanks to Philippe Azoulay for having encouraged us to read Sébastien Mercer. Thanks to Laurence Foguet for the relevance of his suggestions. Thanks to Jean-François Senart for his comments on the individual and society in choral music.

The discussions that took place in a seminar at the Laboratoire des sciences sociales, École normale supérieure, were extremely stimulating. We would like to express our gratitude to its Director Florence Weber, and to our colleagues Tania Angeloff, Cécile Brousse, Jean-Sébastien Eideliman, Jean-Pierre Hassoun and Emmanuelle Saada, whose questions made us reconsider and look at several aspects of our study in greater depth. We have also profited greatly from the questions raised by the *hypokhâgne* students at the Lycée Thiers, Marseille, and from the very pertinent comments that Alain Beitone and Marc Gurgand were kind enough to make about an early version of the manuscript. Thanks, finally, to Olga Baudelot and Colette Establet for their criticisms, comments and suggestions.

Introduction: Suicide and Society

Is there anything new or substantial to be said about suicide, given that sociologists have been around – and have been calculating suicide rates – for one hundred years? Suicide is still, and always has been, an unusual phenomenon, but it is not so unusual as to be considered a purely marginal act. During the past twenty years, the number of suicides in France has put the country amongst the front runners and so has been regarded as a public health problem. In 2000, after an almost continual increase since 1975, the number of suicides reached 11,000 per year, i.e. more than one every hour; this has largely overtaken the number of deaths on the roads, which has been steadily declining during the same period.[1] The number of suicides in France is so high that everyone will, in their lifetime, probably be acquainted, either directly or indirectly, with several suicides amongst people they know. Worldwide, suicide affects approximately one hundred people per hour.

An average rate of 20 per 100,000 is of course equivalent to only a 0.02 per cent chance of committing suicide. This is an infinitely small probability, an amount invisible to the naked eye, for any given year. Suicide is, however, a phenomenon that affects our whole life, even if it does happen only once in any given year. If we base our calculations on a life-span and count the total number of individuals of the same generation who are likely to commit suicide in any given year, we arrive at a higher figure. In France today, there is a 2 per cent possibility that a man aged between 15 and 74 will commit suicide, and there is a 0.7 per cent possibility that a woman will do so.[2] This

---

[1] The number of road accidents in France has fallen steadily from a peak of 18,000 in 1972. The authorities have set themselves the goal of reducing the number to fewer than 5,000 per year.

[2] We arrive at this figure by adding up the annual suicide rates for the generation aged between 15 and 74.

is not a high probability, but it is also not negligible. It is, in any case, much greater than the likelihood of winning the lottery: 0.00031 per cent in any given year, and 0.012 per cent for anyone who buys a lottery ticket twice a week over a period of forty years. Unless we live to a very, very old age, the probability that there will be a lucky winner among the 200 or so people we know personally is infinitesimal: 0.025.

Suicide is a different matter. The strong traumatic charge it carries ensures that the shock wave it generates will spread across an area that is quite disproportionate to its statistical rarity. Mourning following a suicide is not like any other mourning. It is always a 'complicated mourning', to borrow a phrase from the psychiatrist Michel Hanus (2004). Its distinguishing feature is an intense expression of suffering, but also of shock. It is a traumatic form of mourning that lasts longer than other forms and is more likely to generate more depression, anxiety, negative and painful feelings, and feelings of guilt and shame. The scars it leaves on the suicide's close relatives remain indelible. The feeling of guilt it generates is often so painful that it drives some to punish themselves or even to commit suicide in an attempt to assuage their guilt. The suicide's closest relatives are the first to be affected, but the shock waves spread far beyond the inside circle. Because of the questions it raises and precisely because it is such an unusual event, every suicide directly affects a large number of people. Rare events rarely go unnoticed. They make their presence felt because of the way they punctuate the fabric of everyday life.

This is all the more so in that, quite apart from its affective charge, suicide is particularly laden with social meaning. Social anthropologists and sociologists have gradually interpreted it in their own ways.

The contribution of social anthropology

Social anthropology allows us to adopt a new approach to suicide. Some anthropologists have attempted to establish the basic facts by asking people about the deaths of people they know about: such studies have been carried out by Maurice Godelier and Pascal Bonnemère (Bonnemère 1992) in New Guinea, by Charles MacDonald in the Philippines (MacDonald 2003) and by Paul Bohannan in Africa (Bohannan 1967).

How many do you know?

We can get a more accurate idea of how familiar we are with the phenomenon by trying to calculate the number of suicide victims we have known, either directly or indirectly, in the course of our lives; these 'known suicides' involve either people we know or people who are known to people we know. How many times have we rubbed shoulders with suicide by learning of suicides not through the press or the media but by hearing about it from people of our acquaintance, as defined in the broadest sense of the term?

The reader is invited to carry out the experiment for him or herself and to compare the findings with those reached using the very approximate methods of calculation inspired by the sociology of networks. The reader must be careful to spread this exercise over several days, as there are suicides we 'forget about'. . . It is clear that the final score will vary, depending on how old the reader is when he or she carries out the experiment, the social and professional circles in which he or she moves, the extent of his or her social networks, his or her place of residence and so on.

American researchers (Sola Pool 1978; Freeman and Thomson 1989) estimate that we are acquainted with some 5,000 people because we have met them at least once in our lifetime. Given a suicide rate of 21 per 100,000, which is the rate in France today, we should, over a period of forty years, know about forty suicides in our circle of acquaintances.[3] If we restrict the discussion to the more restricted circle of our close acquaintances – a few hundred people, according to the estimates of Alain Degenne and Michel Forsé (1994) – it is highly likely that, over the same period, we will encounter one, two or three cases of suicide. The American Association of Suicidology (2004), in their newsletter written by

---

[3] The result of the calculation is much higher than it would be in our actual experience because it presupposes that the 5,000 people we all know are, on the one hand, equally exposed to the phenomenon (which is not the case) and that we all have access to this representative sample of 5,000 people (which is also not the case), as acquaintanceship networks vary considerably, depending on our social milieu, where we live and so on. This utopian calculation does, however, given an approximate idea of how widespread the phenomenon is and can be compared with the number of suicide victims we can list amongst our acquaintances, defined in the broad sense. For what it is worth, the figure of forty is only slightly higher than that suggested by the personal experience of the authors.

and for survivors of suicide, calculates the extent of the shock wave differently and arrives at a figure of 30,000 suicides per year in the United States.[4] For every suicide victim, there are on average six survivors amongst members of his or her close family – parents, brothers and sisters, husbands and wives, children. A total of 180,000 survivors (6 × 30,000) means that, over fifty generations, some 4.5 million people in the United States have been directly affected by the suicide of someone close to them. The corresponding figures for France appear to affect some 3.6 million individuals, which is equivalent to the active population of the Aquitaine region, the sum total of the nation's senior managers and intellectual professions, or the total population of men and women aged between 55 and 59. That is a lot of people. Whatever the method of calculation used and whatever its degree of inaccuracy, it transpires that suicide cannot be reduced to a statistical exception. The emotional charge it carries and the distance travelled by the shock wave it creates mean that it is a highly visible aspect of social life.

---

[4] Allowance has to be made for the logic of lobbying, which tends to overestimate how far the shock wave travels in order to draw the attention of both individuals and the authorities to the cogency of the work of the lobby in question. Even when revised downwards, the total number of people who are directly affected by one or more suicides is considerable.

Social anthropologists working in the Pacific have drawn attention to female suicides and to the aggressive aspects of the act of suicide. In describing the spectacular suicidal acts of young women, Bronsilaw Malinowski, who is famous for his work on the Melanesians (1926), demonstrates that, in the Trobriand Islands, the suicide involves two psychological motives: it is an expiation of guilt, but also a protest against and revenge upon those who insulted the guilty party in public and forced him or her into an intolerable situation. Historians and social anthropologists who have studied China describe this subtle method for victims of social injustice to take revenge: the suicide of the victim causes the author of the injustice to lose face. This practice is frequently used in China by young women seeking revenge for the oppression they suffer at the hands of their husbands and their in-laws.

In Africa, the social anthropologists associated with Paul Bohannan have paid great attention to the connection between suicide and kinship structures. It appears that individuals very often commit suicide because they find it difficult to fit into the family structure.

Social anthropologists' fieldwork obliges them to take very seriously the collective representations associated with the accounts of their informants, and the moral and social meanings attached to suicide in the various groups they study. In his study of suicide in Singapore (1983), which is at the same time anthropological and sociological, the Australian sociologist Riaz Hassan, who is a South-East Asia specialist, demonstrates, for example, that the differences between the suicide rates of the three ethnic groups making up the population – Chinese, Indian and Malay – must be related to the religious philosophies and world views characteristic of these groups. Amongst the Chinese, suicide is organized around the basic values represented by the concern not to lose face, filial piety, loyalty towards the family, chastity and respect for the elderly. Suicide is a legitimate act when it is the only way to respect these moral values. Indians see things differently. They also prove to be relatively tolerant with regard to suicide: the body is mortal but the soul is immortal and can be reincarnated. The reasons why they commit suicide centre mainly on caste divisions and the family problems that arise between parents and children regarding the choice of marriage partners. In contrast, Malays, who follow the religion of Islam, regard suicide as a refusal to submit to a divinely prescribed order (Islam = submission). More Chinese than Indians commit suicide, but the suicide rate for Malays is close to zero.

Taking 'native theories' into account forces social anthropologists to reconsider the very notion of suicide. Charles MacDonald (2003) summarizes his thoughts about suicide amongst the Palawan as follows:

> In this paper I focus on a type of behaviour or action that is not culturally prescribed – such as the Indian *suttee*, the Japanese *hara-kiri* or the Tao Sung *parang sabil* [. . .]. Theories on suicide do include prescribed suicide (Durkheim used the term 'altruistic'), but for the time being I will not take it into consideration. Prescribed suicide is clearly a very specific behaviour linked with special cultural norms that are absent in the Palawan case [. . .] (425: n 12). The one specific institution documented for the Tao Sung people of Jolo, the *sabil* or *juramentado* [. . .] refers actually to a suicidal attack of the *kamikaze* type, a religiously and politically sanctioned action taking place in the context of warfare or hostile confrontation with a foreign power. It cannot be called simply 'suicide' but has to be defined as 'suicidal homicide' or 'murder-suicide', an act sanctioned by cultural norms, something very different indeed than non-prescribed suicide and self-inflicted death accomplished for personal motives. It makes the *sabil*

culturally similar to collective mass suicides such as those reported in Bali when personal lives were sacrificed in the context of warfare (427–428).

The anthropologist concludes (428) that 'These institutions – *sabil*, *amok* and such – have little to do with the act of suicide as an individual and non-aggressive, non-culturally prescribed type of behaviour, which is the object of the present paper.'

In making this distinction, MacDonald (2003) is taking into consideration the meaning suicides attribute to their acts. The failure to understand the social significance of certain behaviours has done much to make Japan the 'land of suicide', to borrow the title of a Japanese study in demography (*Le Pays du suicide* by Osaki Ayanori, 1960, Tokyo, cited in Duchac 1964). This overall perception makes no distinction between the very high number of ordinary suicides during the immediate post-war period and the very different type of suicides ('voluntary death') prescribed by the cultural institutions (Pinguet 1984).[5] *Seppuku* or *hara-kiri* is a highly codified form of voluntary death and the preserve of the *samurai* class: it is a way of escaping one's enemies in the event of defeat, of following one's leader beyond the grave, of atoning for a sin and responding to an insult in such a way as to provoke a symmetrical act on the part of the offender. These are very precisely ritualized behaviours, and they are inseparable from the code of honour. The *kamikaze* deaths of the Second World War obviously derive from *seppuku*. The literal meaning of the Japanese expression is 'Wind (*kaze*) of the Gods (*kami*)'. The expression appears in the literature and poetry of the tenth century. In 1274 and 1281, two Mongol expeditions threatened Japan with a seaborne invasion. On both occasions, the waves were driven back by typhoons. The Gods caused a wind to blow across the sea that protected the country from invasion. The *kamikaze tobet* is therefore a divine wind that offers protection. On 25 October 1944, Rear Admiral Onishi Taijikiro launched the *Kamikaze Tokubetsu Kogekitai* by loading 500-pound bombs into the noses of Zero fighters whose fuel reserves permitted no going back. Thirty-four ships were sunk and 288 were damaged in 2,000 attacks. The goal was once again to protect the country from a barbarian invasion. Prescribed suicide in the context of a territorial defence mission obviously has nothing in common with ordinary suicide. At the end of the War, when Japan's defeat was complete, Admiral Onishi

---

[5] 'Voluntary death in Japan' is the intentionally neutral title that the writer Maurice Pinguet gives to his historical study (1984) that aims to unravel the origins of the different institutions of *seppuku*, *shinjû* and *kamikaze*.

took his own life in accordance with the ritual forms of *seppuku*, so reinforcing the traditions that had governed his past actions. Japanese tradition also includes another form of voluntary death: the double suicide of lovers, which was widely popularized by Nô theatre. A couple whose passion has been thwarted resolve to die together in a landscape chosen for its beauty and protected by the Buddha Amida. The Japanese call this form of voluntary death *shinjû*, and make a distinction between this and ordinary suicide. In the twentieth century, police officers who compiled registers of deaths certainly included it under suicides. These ritualized forms of voluntary death do not, however, exhaust the topic of suicide in Japan. If we look at police statistics on motives, we find that individual suicides are very different from the prescribed, or at least highly respected, forms of *seppuku* and *shinjû*. 'Pessimism, self-disgust, illness, dementia, worries about the future, anxiety, family conflicts, reprimands, love, poverty, business problems, difficulties in finding work, remorse, debauchery, illegitimate pregnancy, failure at school, ideological reasons' are all reasons for committing suicide listed by the Japanese police in 1955 (Duchac 1964). A European reader who wishes to understand them does not need to refer to anthropological and historical explanations of Japanese institutions. 'Common humanity' is quite enough. And sociologists can begin to compile statistics to find out whether ordinary suicide is more common in Japan than elsewhere.

It isn't society that sheds light on suicide, but rather suicide that sheds light on society

Following sociology's founding father Émile Durkheim, demographers, statisticians and sociologists have indeed explored other ways of studying suicide. Their methods appear to be much cruder than those cited earlier. Having recognized how consistently the phenomenon occurs and the regularity of its variation, these researchers related suicide rates to a relatively limited set of social dimensions: sex, age, occupation, level of income, geographical region, marital status, number of children, month, day of the week, time of day, and so on. Their main investigative tool is statistics. They normally take little or no interest in the meaning that individuals ascribe to their acts, and usually refuse to take into account the reasons given by people who commit suicide. Under these circumstances, do we jettison the work of Durkheim and his successors? The fact that researchers in many countries and from all disciplines constantly show a new interest in his work convinces us that we do not. Of all Durkheim's books, *On Suicide* (1897) is the one that is mostly widely read throughout the world. All those who have taken an interest in suicide in the past hundred years – sociologists, demographers, psychologists, epidemiologists, doctors, psychiatrists – have used the same basic methodology, which has retained the same essential features despite advances in statistics, in order to comment on, verify or invalidate findings. Émile Durkheim has constructed a framework for the analysis of the phenomenon that still allows us to study its variations in every country in the world. The data collected over a period of more than a hundred years by local and national monographs, international comparisons, and anthropological studies of countries that have been overlooked by the statistics have considerably enriched the database established by Durkheim. But we need to understand why there is so much interest in this subject. Suicide is not an unknown phenomenon whose mysteries are dispelled by the statistical scalpel of the sociologists who break it down completely into its various elements, by revealing the social factors that determine it. Society does not shed any light on suicide, but suicide does shed some light on society. It has to be stated quite clearly: the sociology of suicide teaches us nothing about suicide insofar as it is an individual tragedy.

The statistical evidence uncovered by the sociology of suicide does, on the other hand, suggest that we should look at the social factors that either encourage or discourage it. In the vast majority of countries, three to four times fewer women commit suicide than men. In itself, that observation tells us nothing about suicide. But in leading us to ask why women are less vulnerable, it forces us to explore what it is about the social conditions of women and men that is so different as to produce this behavioural difference. Are women more resilient or are men more fragile? Why does the trend towards equality in the social and occupational status of men and women in most developed countries not reduce the gap between their respective suicide rates? What is it about their social status that protects women so constantly? In a word, the sociology of suicide encourages us to ask new questions about being a man or woman in our society. The same is true of all the other variables associated with suicide. For over a century, suicide rates rose regularly with age and were highest amongst the elderly. Since the 1970s, this has no longer been the case in most Western countries, where suicide rates for young people have risen sharply, whilst the rate for old people has fallen steeply. This major shift relates to a fundamental transformation in the social content of different stages of life in our societies. What has happened to our young people since the oil crisis to reduce them to such a state of despair? To take another example of the social rhythms that punctuate our daily lives: despite the romantic representations that depict Sunday as the gloomiest day of the week (*'Je hais les dimanches'* ['I hate Sundays'], sang Juliette Greco, as in the famous song by Damia *Sombre dimanche* ['Gloomy Sunday'], suicide rates are highest on Monday and fall regularly until Sunday, which is when they are at their lowest. It is as though interpersonal relationships grow warmer as the week goes by. How does Monday, the day we go back to work, affect the morale of individuals and the quality of interpersonal relationships? And how does the approach of Sunday help to restore them? The statistical sociology of suicide thus invites us to investigate the nature of the social bond and variations in its intensity. Given that we know that suicide rates vary from society to society, they become sociological symptoms that allow us to identify the distinguishing features of a given society. China is the only country in the world where more women than men commit suicide, especially in the countryside. This draws our attention to the way women are treated by the families into which they marry and, more generally, to the structure of Chinese families.

Suicide: unravelling an enigma

Sociological research into the social changes that accompany variations in suicide rates is therefore a very meaningful exercise, even though we no longer expect it to reveal the 'causes' of suicide, and even though we know that, ultimately, we will neither get to the bottom of it nor find a full explanation. We will in fact never be absolutely certain about the real causal links between social and macroeconomic variables (levels of affluence, unemployment, the social and economic context . . .) and suicide, or in other words between the environment and suicide. The correlations point to concomitant variations, but not to causal chains. If we extend the inquiry worldwide, including all the new demands that would create and also consider temporal series that seem to have little to do with suicide (homicide, alcoholism, per capita GDP), the statistics make it even more difficult to trace the relationship between suicide and society. And, above all, it must not be forgotten that most people do survive in the face of a multiplicity of 'suicidogenic' conditions. Being convinced that social reality does have an effect on suicide, sociologists usually find themselves in a similar position to police investigators faced with an unsolved crime.

They do not have the 'proof' that would allow them to explain everything by confronting the suspect with the evidence, and nor do they have a methodology that might allow them to understand it. They will never get a confession: their certainties have more to do with their inner convictions than with the certainty that comes from the scientific application of proof. They construct hypotheses, accumulate and cross-check clues, and are forced to display great experimental ingenuity. But, at each stage, they learn more about the variables that either favour or discourage suicide (gender, age, urban life . . .) than they do about suicide itself.

There are many puzzles to be solved. Whereas we find a rising suicide rate amongst young people and a falling rate amongst older people in the richest contemporary societies, the opposite trend has been observable in Eastern countries since the collapse of the Soviet bloc. A general trend results in completely different behaviours in the West and in the East. Why?

The validity of statistics on suicide

Statistics provide the sociology of suicide with both its raw material and its primary analytic tool, as other approaches such as observation and interviews cannot really get to grips with it. The reliability of the statistics has been regularly questioned from the nineteenth century onwards. Some critics even argue that the differences observed between women and men, young and old, rich and poor or the cities and the countryside merely reflect the greater ease with which the former categories (women, the young, the rich, cities . . .) avoid appearing in the statistical records, or make suicide look like a different cause of death, in particular accidental death.

Most demographers, sociologists and statisticians of all nationalities are now agreed that, whilst the absolute figures for suicide are inaccurate because they are underestimated, the way the data are broken down by gender, age, place of residence, etc. is still reliable. A study carried out by the Centre d'Épidémiologie sur les Causes Médicales de Décès [Centre for the Epidemiology of Medical Causes of Death], which is part of INSERM [Institut National de la Santé et de la Recherche Médicale: National Institute of Health and Medical Research] and complemented by control surveys undertaken in France concludes that the suicide rates determined by the official statistics are considerably underestimated – by about 20% – but that correcting them does little to change the sociodemographic and geographical characteristics of suicide.

The control surveys also show that attempted suicide and 'successful' suicide are two different phenomena because of the demographic and social characteristics of the individuals involved. Although they represent the majority of attempted suicides, women, intellectuals and townspeople are the categories least likely to commit suicide. Attempted suicides peak at weekends, whereas successful suicide bids peak on Mondays; Fridays, Saturdays and Sundays are the days when 'successful' suicides are least common.

For further information on the reliability of the statistics on suicide, criticisms of them, and on how best to use them, see Baudelot and Establet (1999), Douglas (1967), and Jougla, Pequignot, Chappert, Rossolin, Le Toullec and Pavillon (2002).

Similarly, the relationship between suicide and wealth is not as simplistic as Durkheim beleived. At first sight, suicide is more common in the richest countries, but it is not the rich who kill themselves in those countries. Whilst there is, in any given year, a correlation between suicide and wealth in various countries, temporal variations in suicide rates are not automatically in line with economic growth. Why not?

In one of his most brilliant analyses, Durkheim puts his finger on the contradictions of conjugal society. But he refuses to take them into consideration. There is a close correlation between divorce and suicide. But the effects of the rising divorce rate are not restricted to divorced people. In societies where divorce is more common, married men are less protected from suicide, whilst married women are more protected. In extreme cases, married men are less protected than single men. We therefore have to look at the evolution of conjugal society in terms of contradictions and probably reveal the inequalities between men and women that exist in traditional relationships. Suicide can therefore shed light on the conflict-ridden nature of the social bond, and remind us that conflict can be a source of cohesion. Wars, when cohesion becomes greater on both sides, provide a classic example.

A society is not just a demographic juxtaposition of segments or an economic synergy of resources, and still less is it a premeditated construct that is built in accordance with juridical rules and political conventions. A society is a way of being together. It is something that is alive, and therefore mysterious. A society is, to use Durkheim's favourite expression, a reality *sui generis*. It can neither be reduced to the effects of a voluntaristic or utilitarian construct, nor broken down into its component elements. The immediate opacity of society is coterminous with its reality. That is why we can expect a great deal from the meticulous and organized observation – *à la Durkheim* – of the connections that are woven between the macroscopic transformations of society and the unusual and significant phenomenon of suicide.

In order to attempt to synthesize the vast amount of data that have been collected and analysed over the last hundred years and more, we will take as a starting point an approach that is both decisive and marginal in Durkheim's own work: the relationship between suicide and wealth. Durkheim was writing at the end of a century of economic growth that humanity had never experienced before. And if we read him today, we are well aware that the process has accelerated still further. In Durkheim's work, most of the social phenomena he studies in relation to suicide are almost directly related to the rapid enrichment of European societies (urbanization, changes in the rate of fertility, changes in religious practices, rising divorce rates . . .). And yet Durkheim makes only a lateral study of the relationship between suicide and wealth in order to advance the interesting and paradoxical thesis that 'poverty protects'. Whilst we will not overlook the connection between suicide, age, gender and urbanization, we will make wealth and its growth central to our analysis.

Surprise, surprise: the contemporary data simply do not confirm Durkheim's diagnosis. This is not simply because of the growth of sociological knowledge or because the data are better, but because of the profound transformations that have taken place in the relationship between suicide and social phenomena. There is only a very partial overlap between the social picture of suicide in the nineteenth century and in the twentieth.

1 Does Poverty Protect?

If we think about it, the relationship between wealth and suicide is not easy to disentangle purely on the basis of what we remember and what we have read. Indian newspapers are full of stories about peasants who commit suicide because they are crippled with debts. Chinese papers are full of stories about poor young women from the country who swallow weedkiller because they are being overexploited by their mothers-in-law. The young American boy of Indian origin from Minnesota who, in March 2005, massacred his classmates before taking his own life had seen two of his grandparents commit suicide and was not rolling in money. In France, the men who shoot their wives and children and then turn their guns on themselves in despair are more likely to be living on income support [*RMI: Revenu Minimum d'Insertion*] than paying tax on wealth [*ISF: Impôt sur la Fortune*]; i.e. they are poor. It is possible to imagine a whole scenario that leads from poverty, and especially sudden poverty, to despair and all the behaviours it entails: rebellion, escape through drink or drugs, and suicide. We can superimpose on these images, which do sometimes correspond to reality, other images that are very different but just as real.

It is possible to be heir to the throne of Denmark and still ask the whole world about the meaning of life. A former Prime Minister who has no financial worries puts a bullet in his brain. It is well known, perhaps too well known, that Japan is a country where suicide is common: however, it is neither a poor country nor a country where poverty is rife. There has been a lot of glib talk about the case of Sweden. During the *Trente Glorieuses*,[1] the 'Swedish model' was the

---

[1] Literally, the 'thirty glorious years': the period of reconstruction and growth between 1946 and 1975. The expression, which has become canonical, derives from the title of Jean Fourastié's *Les Trente Glorieuses, ou La Révolution invisible de 1946 à 1975* (Paris: Fayard, 1979) [translator].

envy of the countries of southern Europe because of the balance that had been struck between justice and efficiency, and because of the freedom of relations between the sexes. And yet Swedish cinema, which was the height of fashion in France and elsewhere, was overshadowed by an existential angst that affected every aspect of life. *She Only Danced One Summer* (a Swedish film made by Arne Mattsson in 1951) dealt with love and sexuality with unprecedented daring and had all Europe's frustrated adolescents flocking to the cinema: the film ended with a fatal accident that looked like retribution. *Wild Strawberries* (Ingmar Bergman, 1957) is about a celebrated professor who revisits the places of his past with the disillusioned feeling that he has never escaped his loneliness. Bergman is Sweden's most famous film maker, and all his work centres on relationships that break down, the obsessive fear of loneliness and the failure of men and women, and children and adults, to understand each other. As a result, wealth, social justice and individual freedom become synonymous with boredom and lead to existential angst. Paradoxically, the Latin peoples of southern Europe seem to gain their vitality from outsmarting taboos, evading taxes, struggling with unemployment and getting around the law. *A Latin or a catholic paradox?* A publication in the *Réalités* series that introduces readers to the 'wonders of Europe' expresses this quite candidly (*Les Merveilles de l'Europe*, Paris: Hachette, 1963: 174):

> Being melancholic and meditative by nature, it is claimed that the Swedes suffer from a disquiet of the soul. From August Strindberg to Ingmar Bergman, artists have struggled to find a name for the nostalgic despair that sometimes overcomes them, especially when they see the crystal landscapes of Sweden. Perhaps all that this society, which is the most organized, the most caring, the most restrained and the most stubborn society in the world, needs to make it completely happy is some sunshine.

The text is illustrated with a photograph of a gorgeous Swedish girl. And it is a well-known fact that suicide is not common in the Islamic countries, most of which are poor.

Suicide and wealth around the world

We can begin to get some idea of the relationship between suicide and wealth by drawing a very simple graph showing the value of the average wealth of each country, as measured by per capita GDP (Gross Domestic Product) and that of its suicide rate. For the moment, the discussion will be restricted to the male suicide rate, which is usually higher.[2]

If we look at Fig. 1.1 (page 16), we can see two clouds: a vertical cumulonimbus on the left that rises above Romania and the Czech Republic and includes almost every country in the former Soviet bloc, and a stratocumulus that gently rises along the horizontal axis and that includes every known country in the world, from Egypt to Switzerland. The cumulonimbus formed by the Soviet-bloc countries shows that we have here a group of relatively poor countries with high suicide rates. In terms of per capita GDP, these are amongst the poorest countries. GDP is a measure of wealth available on the market, and it underestimates wealth that is freely available – such as health and education. If we took that into account, the cumulonimbus associated with the former socialist bloc would move towards the right of our graph above Chile and South Korea. The cloud would not, however, merge into the rest of the picture. The conclusion is obvious: no matter which criterion we use to measure their wealth, the countries of the former socialist bloc have abnormally high suicide rates. They deserve particular study.

If we focus on the stratocumulus that gently rises along the horizontal axis, we may assume that suicide rates rise along with wealth. If we ignore the cumulonimbus countries, that impression becomes more pronounced. There is a definite tendency, represented by the straight line, for suicide to be associated with wealth. If we look carefully at the graph, we see that, given their level of wealth, Japan and Sweden have relatively low suicide rates: they are below that line. On the other hand, certain countries more rarely discussed in this connection have suicide rates that are higher than their level of development might suggest: they are above the line. They are, in order of affluence, New Zealand, Canada, Germany, Belgium, Finland, Austria, France and Switzerland.

If, however, we overlook these exceptions, the general trend is clearly visible. The richer the country, the higher its suicide rate. We might therefore attribute high rates of suicide to either wealth itself (idleness, boredom, the satisfaction of all possible desires . . .) or to one or more of the social realities that are usually associated with wealth: urbanization, competitiveness, the rise of individualism, ageing populations . . .

[2] Sources: WHO 1997, 1999. The relationship between suicide and 'gender' is examined in Chapter 9 below.

Figure 1.1 Male suicide rates and GDP

Sources: World Health Organization, 1995; United Nations Development Programme (UNDP), 1997.

Suicide rates are lowest in the poorest countries: Egypt, Peru, Syria, Nicaragua, Ecuador, China and even India. The African countries are not represented, as there are no data on suicide there. Suicides do, however, occur in Africa. The studies coordinated by Paul Bohannan (1967) for Nigeria, Uganda and Kenya are proof of this. When we calculate them for certain populations, the rates are low: they vary between 5 and 10 per 100,000. We might therefore agree with Durkheim that 'poverty protects'. Variations in the rate of suicide appear to provide a sort of moral compensation for the miserable inequalities of wealth in the world. *Ex egestate nascitur virtus*: virtue is born of poverty.

In rich countries, it is in poor areas that suicide occurs

This moralistic vision is not, however, borne out by the statistics for the richest countries. In these countries, the suicide rate is highest in the poorest suburbs, not in the city centres. In the United States, the most urbanized and richest states – those around Chicago, San Francisco, Los Angeles and New York – have the lowest suicide rates, whilst suicide is most common in the poorest states that are least representative of the 'American way of life'. Within the United States, suicide rates are inversely proportional to wealth.

And it is Manchester and Birmingham, cities that have been ravaged by the decline of industry and made famous in the films of Ken Loach, that have the highest suicide rates in Great Britain. In France, it is the richest *départements* that have the lowest suicide rates. The same is true of Japan's 42 prefectures. And wherever statistics on the occupations of suicides are available, we find that suicide is most common at the bottom of the social ladder. We will come back to this point.

The statistics bring us up against a contradiction: if we believe the international statistics, we can readily conclude that wealth has an enormous impact on suicide. Economic development appears to lead, either directly or indirectly, to dissatisfaction with life and to the despair caused by the moral forces most directly associated with progress. That is quite in keeping with the explanations and preoccupations of Durkheim, who found in the development of the modern societies of the late nineteenth century 'suicidogenic currents', many of them fuelled by the loss of protection once provided by traditional communities such as parishes, families and villages – and by the growing autonomy of individual initiatives whose aspirations were growing unchecked in every domain of life, including wealth, sexuality and thoughts. But the national data available for the richest countries demonstrate precisely the opposite: suicide is most common in those regions and social categories that have been left behind by progress.

Are there growing inequalities?

A quick way of solving this problem might be to assume that the most highly developed societies are also the societies that develop the greatest inequalities. This thesis tends to be supported by Corrado Gini, who developed one of the most reliable measures of the concentration of wealth. Using Austro-Hungarian and Italian data from the late nineteenth and early twentieth centuries, Gini found that the development of modern capitalist and industrial society reinforced the concentration of wealth by transforming its base: the most obvious effect of social revolutions was to create sudden impoverishment as well as sudden enrichment. Inspired by the work of Gini, Franco Savorgnan, an Italian professor of political economy, clearly demonstrated (1930) that there was a growth in the concentration of wealth in Austria between 1903 and 1910. This sweeping diachronic evaluation was confirmed by a series of snapshots from 1908 that apparently demonstrated that the concentration of wealth was greatest in the richest regions and the largest cities; the same contrast could be observed between provincial capitals and the provinces themselves. The rising value of financial investments and of urban land went hand in hand with the ruin of the countryside, the impoverishment of the peasants and the replacement of the ruling elites. Gini measured the concentration of wealth simply by calculating the percentage of the population that monopolized a given percentage of overall social wealth. When wealth is distributed equally, Gini's coefficient equals 0, and when all wealth is monopolized by a tiny fraction of the population, the coefficient is 1. The nearer the coefficient is to 1, the more wealth is concentrated. This is a very effective measure as it is independent of the initial measure of wealth, be it the dollar, rupee or the medieval French *livre tournois*.

If economic development had followed the trend identified by Gini at the beginning of the twentieth century, we would have an easy explanation of the statistics of suicide. Development leads to an increase in average wealth but it increases inequalities. If we dusted down Durkheim's theory a little, we would have a clear and distinct explanation that is perfectly in tune with the common sociological complaints about the fate of neo-liberal societies. Development makes it increasingly possible to satisfy needs, but it heightens aspirations still further and, as the discrepancy between the resources available at the top and the bottom of the social pyramid, there is a growing gulf between desire and reality at the bottom.

Unfortunately for this ingenious hypothesis, the path of development in the twentieth century has not followed the ups and downs seen by Gini. In the richest countries, the concentration of consumption, income and even wealth tends to decrease over time. And, in any given period, the concentration of wealth falls as the country becomes richer.

Table 1.1 (page 20) which was compiled at the end of the twentieth century, clearly shows that the concentration of income decreases regularly as wealth increases. The poorest and most unequal countries include all the countries of Latin America and many African countries. These are all countries with a very low suicide rate. In contrast, most of the countries of the former Socialist bloc figure amongst the poorest countries and have a low level of inequality.[3] And as we have seen, all these countries have high suicide rates. In northern countries, where suicide rates are generally high, the distribution of wealth is quite even. One thing at least is clear: growing social inequality is not a tenable explanation.

All the national statistics on the evolution of wealth confirm this late twentieth-century snapshot. This was one of the main findings of the international symposium organized by the CNRS (Centre national de la recherche scientifique) in 1978 (Kessler, Masson and Strauss-Kahn 1982). Between 1953 and 1973, the share of the richest fell slightly in the United States. Taussig verified this finding from 1922 onwards. The most convincing demonstration is provided by Atkinson *et al*'s study of Great Britain between 1922 and 1972. In 1929, Corrado Gini (1931) himself estimated the concentration of wealth in France to be 0.84; in 1986, the index fell to 0.66,[4] and in 1991 it fell to 0.63.[5]

---

[3] These minor differences in wealth arise from these countries' socialist heritage on the one hand, and from the fact that their average wealth is calculated in purely market terms on the other.

[4] Calculation based on data supplied by Lollivier and Verger (1990).

[5] Calculation based on data supplied by Guillaumat-Taillet, Malpot and Paquel (1996).

Table 1.1   Concentration of wealth (1995)

	low	average	high
	6 countries	16 countries	15 countries
Per capita GDP low	Rwanda, Pakistan, Mongolia, Burundi, Uzbekistan, Yemen	Bangladesh, Vietnam, Nepal, Ivory Coast, Laos, Mauritania, Uganda, India, Tanzania, Mozambique, Ghana, Ethiopia, Guinea, Cambodia, Moldova, Senegal	Armenia, Kenya, Madagascar, Gambia, Burkina, Mali, Niger, Nigeria, Zambia, Lesotho, Guinea-Bissau, Bolivia, Honduras, Nicaragua, Papua New Guinea
	9 countries	13 countries	15 countries
Per capita GDP average	Belarus, Bulgaria, Rumania, Egypt, Ukraine, Indonesia, Latvia, Lithuania, Croatia	Sri Lanka, Algeria, Kazakhstan, Azerbaijan, Jamaica, Jordan, Georgia, Morocco, Guyana, China, Kirghistan, Turkmenistan, Thailand	Turkey, Tunisia, Ecuador, Philippines, Peru, Dominican Republic, Panama, Venezuela, Salvador, Guatemala, Zimbabwe, Columbia, Paraguay, Brazil, Swaziland
	22 countries	8 countries	7 countries
Per capita GDP high	Slovakia, Austria, Hungary, Denmark, Japan, Sweden, Belgium, Czech Republic, Finland, Norway, Luxemburg, Italy, Slovenia, Germany, Canada, Poland, South Korea, Spain, Netherlands, Greece, France, Switzerland	Australia, Israel, Portugal, Ireland, Great Britain, Estonia, Trinidad and Tobago, United States	Uruguay, Costa Rica, Russia, Malaysia, Mexico, Chile, South Africa

Source: UNDP, *Rapport mondial sur le développement humain 2001*, tables 1 and 12.

Recent statistics confirms that the gap within rich countries decreases as wealth increases. In France, the ratio of the average income to the average working-class wage rose from 100 to 130 between 1900 and 1998. This certainly represents an increase in inequality, but it is a relatively small increase when spread over a period of one hundred years.[6] On the other hand, the evolution of the concentration of wealth over the last century has been characterized by a sharp fall in inequality. Whereas the richest 10% monopolized 45% of all taxable income in 1900, they owned little more than 43% in 1938, 32% in 1950, 36% in 1960, 31% in 1980 and 32% in 1998 (Atkinson, Glaude, Olier and Piketty, 2001).

The statistics therefore stubbornly resist the apparently attractive hypothesis that attributes the rise in the suicide rate in rich countries to growing inequalities within them.

A further paradox completely destroys the basis of this hypothesis. Whilst, as we have seen, inequalities lessen within any given country as it becomes richer, inequalities between the richest and the poorest countries tend, on the contrary, to increase in spectacular fashion at the international level. In 1960, 20% of the richest countries owned 70.2% of the world's wealth. They owned 73.9% in 1970, 76.9% in 1980, and 82.7% in 1989. Over the last forty years, Gini's index has gone from 0.69 to 0.87. To use another measure: the average gap between the poorest 20% and the richest 20% rose from 1 to 30 in 1960, from 1 to 32 in 1970, from 1 to 45 in 1980 and from 1 to 59 in 1989 (UNDP annual reports). Contrary to all expectations, the suicide rate is lowest in the poor countries, even though they are also the countries in which the wealth gap is now the greatest.

The relationship between suicide and wealth is therefore proving to be more complex than it at first seemed. The only way to resolve this enigma is to take a step at a time and follow the path of history. We can then reveal the considerable differences that exist between the pattern of suicide in the nineteenth century and in the twentieth.

---

[6] The difference between average wages in 1900 and 1998 is largely explained by the growing proportion of managerial staff [cadres] in the wage-earning population.

2 Take-off . . .

It can be said that there is a general relationship between a country's wealth and its suicide rate. The richer the country, the more suicides there are. The discovery of this relationship, which is well founded on the basis of macroeconomic data for many countries in a given year, is a first finding. But as such it raises more problems than it resolves. For the moment, we are merely talking about a ratio – seen from afar – between two statistical magnitudes: the gross domestic product (GDP), on the one hand, and the suicide rate on the other. How national wealth influences or does not influence the suicide of individuals remains a complete enigma. If we wish to get a clearer view, the only thing to do is to proceed one step at a time. For the moment, we will retain the same analytic tool – the relationship between the suicide rate and GDP – but we will change the scale of our observations in terms of both space and time. We will abandon the global point of view and examine the relationship country by country. We will abandon the synchronic approach – a snapshot picture of the close correlation between wealth and suicide in any given year – and explore the relationship in historical terms. Has it always been this way?

No: if we turn to history, we find that the ratio between these two magnitudes is not the same in the nineteenth and twentieth centuries. In the nineteenth century, things are quite clear: the link between growing wealth and suicide is positive and well established. Things are much less clear in the twentieth century.

Between the 1830s, when the first statistics were published, and the eve of the First World War, suicide rates rose steeply in the vast majority of European countries. This increase in the phenomenon went hand in hand with spectacular economic development. This increase would be observed in almost all countries, regardless of the level of their suicide rates. Italy and Great Britain, where rates were

Figure 2.1   Evolution of suicide rates and GDP, 1871–1913 (base 100 in 1871), France

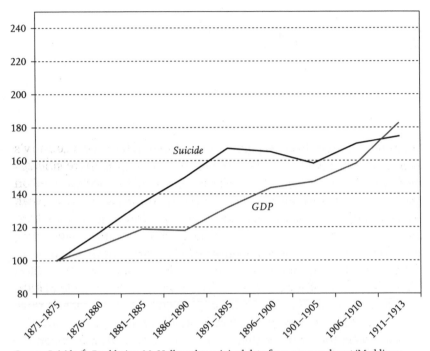

Source: Suicide, É. Durkheim, M. Halbwachs; original data from www.ggdc.net/Maddison.

low, saw their suicide rates rise by 2.5 and 1.6, respectively, between 1870 and 1914. The same was true of countries whose suicide rates were higher to begin with: France, Belgium, Sweden, Austria and the Netherlands. With the exception of Norway and Denmark, there was a positive and close correlation between the growth of wealth and the rising suicide rate in all countries between 1870 and 1914. Suicide rates and national wealth rose at the same rate. Figures 2.1, 2.2 and 2.3 demonstrate this quite clearly for France, Great Britain and Italy: the growth of GDP is shown in bold, and the rising suicide rate in a light tint rule.

It was precisely this relationship that most troubled Durkheim. The period in which he wrote *On Suicide* was a period of accelerated growth in all European countries and America. It brought about a whole series of social transformations: the growth of cities, the introduction of modern transport, roads and railways, the exodus from the countryside, and the expansion of both industry and the market economy. Per capita output rose more rapidly than it had done over the previous fifty decades. Under these circumstances, it is logical to conclude that an increase in wealth is the direct or indirect cause of suicide. This impression is confirmed by the geographical distribution of suicide within each of these countries. In France, suicide peaked in those regions where economic development was most dynamic: the Parisian basin and the urbanized *départements* (Rhône, Bouches-du-Rhône). The rural regions, in contrast, were spared. The big cities, where the effects of modern social structures were both concentrated and cumulative, were the places where suicide did most damage. This contrast between the cities and the countryside is very widespread: it is also observable in Sweden, Czechoslovakia, Belgium, Russia, Germany, Hungary, Austria, the United States and Italy. When he discusses the link Durkheim established between suicide and religious faith, Maurice Halbwachs (1930: 184–187) is constantly drawn to the link between suicide and urban society: the Protestant is not just a Protestant, but also someone who lives in an urban environment and, conversely, the Catholic is also someone who lives in the country.[1] When we now measure the correlation between per capita GDP and the contemporary suicide rate in the light of our improved data, we still find a very close relationship between the two. It therefore seems that economic development and in particular new forms of social organization are indeed responsible for the rise in suicide rates.

Durkheim was so convinced that this was the case that his famous study *On Suicide*, which was published in 1897 at a time when France's suicide rate reached one of its historical peaks, looks, in its very controlled methodology, like an attempt to exorcize his anxiety. The large-scale economic and social transformations that were setting free the forces available for the industrial division of labour appear to him to be making individuals weaker. The rapid development of individualism, the spirit of free inquiry, a diversified economy and freedom of choice within what was still a familiar society were all possible causes of a dizzying rise in suicides rates and Durkheim charts it in table after table. The anxiety caused by his statistical findings was all the more intense in that Durkheim was in no sense a sociologist who was nostalgic for the past. On the

---

[1] Maurice Halbwachs was Émile Durkheim's disciple and collaborator. Born in 1877, he died in Buchenwald in 1945. In 1930, he published his *Les Causes du suicide*, which continues Durkheim's work but takes issue with it over certain points.

Figure 2.2   Evolution of suicide rates and GDP, 1871–1913 (base 100 in 1871), Great Britain

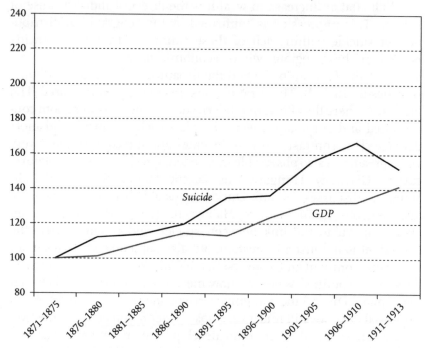

Source: Suicide, É. Durkheim, M. Halbwachs; original data from www.ggdc.net/Maddison.

contrary, he had every sympathy for most of the trends towards greater emancipation and affluence that characterize modern societies. Durkheim was not a disgruntled man who was nostalgic for the good old days and he often referred to the blinkered effects of 'misoneism', especially in education.

One very moving text shows the great value Durkheim attributed to what he calls organic solidarity, in other words the individualized basis of modern society. I refer to his intervention in the Dreyfus affair (1898: 50–52), in which he sings the praises of individualism or the 'necessary doctrine':

> Not only is individualism not anarchical, but it is henceforth the only system of beliefs which can ensure the moral nature of the country . . . For in order to halt its advance it would be necessary to prevent men from differentiating between themselves more and more, to equalize their personalities, to lead them back to the old conformism of former times, to contain, as a result, the tendency for societies to

Figure 2.3　Evolution of suicide rates and GDP, 1871–1913 (base 100 in 1871), Italy

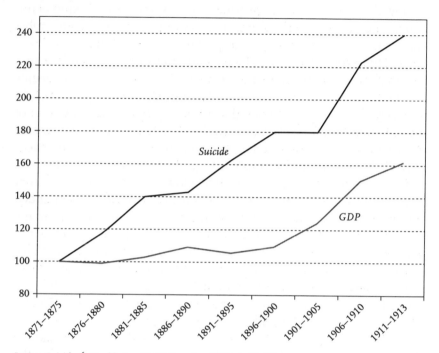

Source: Suicide, É. Durkheim, M. Halbwachs; GDP, A. Maddison.

become always more extended and more centralized and to place an obstacle in the way of the increasing process of the division of labour. Such an enterprise, whether desirable or not, infinitely exceeds all human capability.

He justifies his intervention at length and on scientific grounds. A sociologist has to recall that, in the society in which we live, the rights of the individual who is on trial – the presumption of innocence, the need for proof and the right to a defence – outweigh the interests of the state and its organs. Rather as though he were replying to Paul Valéry, who adorned an anti-Dreyfus petition with the slogan 'I prefer injustice to disorder', Emile Durkheim mobilizes all his sociological knowledge to demonstrate, that precisely, in the France of his day, disorder was injustice. Durkheim was by no means an antimilitarist. He showed it during the 1914–1918 War by joining a group of nationalist intellectuals. His attitude towards Dreyfus was in no sense dictated by his Jewish origins. Like those

Jews who sided with Dreyfus, Durkheim defended him in the name of universal sociological values.[2]

Now the society that had provided the basis for his thinking about ethics and his political commitment was proving to be the most anxiogenic of societies, since the suicide rate was rising as it developed. This explains the sociologist's attempt to find an answer to a fact that posed a threat to the society to which he was so deeply attached. There was no question of going back to the past, even in intellectual terms, to societies that imposed their norms in spite of individual differences, even though the statistics showed that suicide rates were lowest in forgotten backwaters and rural societies, in places were Catholicism was the dominant creed and in poor countries.

The economic transformations that allowed the nineteenth century to accumulate wealth on an unprecedented scale obviously demanded and brought about huge changes in behaviours, values and thinking. It was these moral changes, which gave individuals and individual initiatives a much greater part to play, that could provide a justifiable explanation for the increase in suicide. Other countries are now going through the turbulent transformations of economic and social life that the countries of Europe experienced in the nineteenth century. This is especially true of India and China, whose growth rates, which are much higher than those of European societies during their take-off stage, are also paralleled by great changes in economic life and in the transition to a market economy. Does the impressive increase in the national wealth of these two countries go hand in hand with a concomitant rise in the suicide rate?

India, 1950–2000: an economic giant is born and suicide takes off

In the case of India, the answer is a clear 'yes'. In India, suicide has become officially recognized as a public health problem. According to the National Crime Records Bureau, the rate of suicide, as measured by official statistics and probably underestimated on a national scale, rose from 6.8 to 9.9 per 100,000 during the ten years from 1985 to 1995 (Kumar 1995; Mayer and Ziaian 2002).

On the whole, the picture of suicide in the Indian subcontinent does evoke the nineteenth-century trends that gave Durkheim food for

---

[2] The point is made very clearly in Daniel Panzac's book (2003: 90–91) in a very lucid statement by Léon Blum.

Table 2.1 India: suicide rates per 100,000 calculated by gender and level of education (2000)

	Men	Women
Illiterate	8.4	5.0
Primary	9.7	8.9
Middle	22.7	20.9
Secondary or higher	19.8	18.4
Total	12.8	8.8

thought. The highest suicide rates were recorded in those towns that developed as the result of accelerated industrial revolutions following independence: Bangalore, 30.3; Indore, 30.1; Nagpur, 22.1; Coimbatore, 20.1; Kanpur, 21.4: Bhopal, 18.3; Poona, 13.4; and Jaipur, 13.4.

With the exception of Jaipur, none of these cities is on the classic tourist trail. In the space of a few years, Bangalore has become the capital of India's Silicon Valley, having once been a comfortable British garrison town and a real garden city, full of golf courses and tennis courts. Indore is a big centre for the textile industry and one of the motor industry's capitals. Nagpur is the headquarters of many multinationals. Kanpur makes a living from the aviation and chemical industries and from the agricultural industry. Coimbatore makes its living from hydroelectricity. Bhopal, as is well known, was the site of an industrial crime against humanity (1984). These cities are a reminder that India is not just 'Bollywood, maharajas, poverty and spirituality'. It is the industrialized India caught up in globalization that is experiencing the highest suicide rates. As in nineteenth-century Europe, there is a positive correlation (0.30) between these countries' per capita wealth and their suicide rates. There is also a further index: the suicide rate rises as levels of education improve.

Having read Durkheim, we have no difficulty in understanding the reasons for India's rising suicide rate at the end of the twentieth century. Indian scientists have also been struck by the contrast between economic development and suicide rates in the southern states, which are the richest in the subcontinent. Commenting on Professor Nataraj's report to Congress, V. Shridar remarks that development in itself does not appear to do anything to protect societies.[3] Suicide rates are at their highest in southern states such as Kerala

[3] V. Shridar is Senior Economist at the Madras Institute of Development Studies. The same points and observations are made by Halliburton (1998).

(30.5), Karnataka (24.2), Tamil Nadu (18.6) and especially Pondichéry, which has the distinction of having the highest suicide rate in the country. This seems paradoxical in a context where the people of these states have a high degree of access to social sector amenities, in particular health and education. Nataraj suggests that the social characteristics of these states may explain the paradox. He notes that these societies are more heterogeneous and that their inhabitants have higher aspirations. In addition, links between town and countryside are more frequent and facilitate a wider propagation of urban values and the media. According to Nataraj, the fact that the market as an institution has penetrated these states more comprehensively is also a key factor. He points out that Kerala is in direct contact with the world market: many people from Kerala work in the Gulf and agriculture is dominated by plantations. The same point is made by articles devoted to suicide amongst farmers, which is usually associated with high levels of debt (Parthasarathy 1998; Prassad 1999). These things all expose society to a greater instability and insecurity.

Two Australian authors (Mayer and Ziaian 2002) confirm on the basis of very reliable statistics the existence of a very strong link between economic growth and the Indian subcontinent's suicide rate. Intrigued by the fact that marriage offers Indian women little protection, they attempt to identify – all other things being equal – the factors that do most to encourage suicide. They identify three specific variables that go a long way towards explaining the high male rates of suicide: the degree of industrialization, which they measure in terms of electricity consumption, increased life expectancy and, above all, rising standards of education. Suicide is most common amongst the most highly educated categories. All these correlations paint a picture of suicide very similar to that traced by Durkheim in late nineteenth-century Europe. The sudden transformation of social relations brought about by the rapid development of a market economy gives individuals considerably more autonomy. They are left alone in charge of their own lives, and no longer enjoy the support and assistance of traditional communities. The best-educated individuals are precisely those individuals who have done most to free themselves, through knowledge and reason, from the grip of collective structures by accumulating the personal knowledge and skills that allow them to live and act autonomously. As they become more individualized, they also become more vulnerable. Education is both a cause and an effect of individualism.

1980–2000: China awakens and suicide rates rise

What about China? China, too, has definitely 'woken up'. For the last fifteen or so years China has been experiencing the heavy turbulence of economic take-off on a grand scale. Is this take-off having the same effects on the suicide rate as economic take-off in nineteenth-century Europe and contemporary India?

The findings are less clear because there are a number of gaps in the statistical records. The first reforms to trigger economic development in a market economy date from 1978. However, reliable statistics on causes of death only begin in 1987. Whilst the available data for the period 1987–1999 reveal that the phenomenon was remarkably stable, with a suicide rate of about 13 or 14 per 100,000 men and 14 to 17 per 100,000 women, these statistics are flawed by a bias that detracts greatly from their quality. An article published in the British journal *The Lancet* in 2002 by a professor in Harvard's Department of Social Medicine and two Chinese researchers working at Beijing's Centre for Suicide Research and Prevention casts doubt on and corrects the figures published in the World Health Organization's series (Phillips, Li and Zhang 2002). Like many other countries, China does not base its figures on a comprehensive of record of deaths from suicide. The statistics on causes of death are based on a cautious sample of only 10% of the population – already covering more than 100 million individuals! The sample was, however, drawn from zones that were able to collect reliable and well organized data, with the result that urban areas are over-represented. This bias is especially significant where suicide is concerned because, on the basis of the available data, suicides are three times more common in the countryside than in the cities. This initial bias causes the official statistics to seriously underestimate the suicide rate. There is also a second bias: the proportion of suicides that are stated to result from 'unknown causes' and that are not classified as 'suicide'. We also find that there are major variations when it comes to estimating the scale of the phenomenon, depending on which sources are used. The figures supplied by the Chinese Ministry of Health for WHO's Statistical Yearbook are the lowest: 250,000 suicides per year. Those published in the study carried out by the Global Burden of Disease rise to 343,000 cases (equivalent to a suicide rate of 30.3 per 100,000 for 1990), whilst the *World Health Report* records 413,000 suicides for 1998 alone (a suicide rate of 32.9). The differences can be explained in terms of the methods of data collection used and the way they have been adjusted on the basis of observations made in various parts of the territory by the health survey network established by the Chinese Academy of Preventive Medicine (China's Disease Surveillance Point System).

The authors of the *Lancet* study make a new estimate of Chinese suicide rates for the period 1995–1999 by correcting the bias which, in their view, flaws not only the official data published by the Ministry, which underestimates the extent of the phenomenon, but also the other two studies, which tend to overestimate it. They correct the official statistics, providing a new balance between cities and the countryside, and reallocate cases in which suicide is accepted to be the cause of death but which are not recorded under the relevant categories of age, gender and place of residence. They then demonstrate that the method used by the other two bodies to reclassify cases of deaths from unknown causes and especially 'other cases of violent death' or 'accidental death from unknown cause' tend to overestimate the cases of suicide because their reclassification system is over-generous. They also explain the discrepancies between the sources by resorting to different criteria for the distinction between rural and urban zones. After these considerations and as a result of their new weightings, they reach what seems to them to be a reasonable estimate: an average rate of 23.2 suicides per 100,000 for the period 1995–1999. This rate is higher than that for France during the same period.

Whatever the recorded variations between the sources may be, the Chinese suicide rate is now at a high level. The Ministry for Health in fact recognizes that suicide is China's fourth greatest public health problem, given that it accounts for 4.4% of all deaths in the country. It is the fourth highest cause of deaths amongst women in the countryside, and the eighth highest for women in the cities, the eighth highest for men in the countryside, and the fourteenth for men in urban areas. Suicide is the major cause of death amongst Chinese people aged between 15 and 34, and it is responsible for 19% of all deaths in that age group. In rural areas, the mortality rate from suicide amongst young women is more than seven times higher than the rate of deaths from medical complications during pregnancy, childbirth or post-partum infections. The equivalent ratio is 37.8 to 5.2 per 100,000.

The link between the extent of the phenomenon and the strength of economic development has yet to be determined. The absence of long statistical series precludes an unambiguous answer. The data available for other Asian countries for which we have reliable statistical series and for the countries of Eastern Europe reveal major fluctuations in suicide rates, which appear to be in line with social and economic transformations there. It is therefore probable that the profound transformations in the economic infrastructure and in social life that are leading to China's 'modernization' do have an effect on the suicide rate. But in what way? Have political stability and economic prosperity helped to lower the suicide rate since the time of the Cultural Revolution, when it is suspected that it peaked? Or has it risen as a result of the new pressures brought to bear by economic reforms? No one can reach a definite conclusion on the basis of the available data. One thing is certain, however, and it may point to a link between the suicide rate and economic growth in modern China: millions and millions of Chinese now make up 'floating populations'. Displaced *en masse* from their villages to urban building sites or industrial plants, their deaths are still registered in the rural communes from which they come. A more accurate picture of suicide rates amongst these categories of migrants, who have been brutally brought face to face with an economic and social world that is completely different to their own, might shed further light on the link between modern China's very high suicide rate and its dizzying rate of growth.

These three sets of data – Europe in the nineteenth century and India and China in the twentieth – seem to confirm perfectly Durkheim's analyses and predictions. In his view, modernity results in individualism, and individualism results in suicide. If we supplement Durkheim's sociological analysis with its economic backdrop, we do no more than reveal a further explanatory dimension: economic development leads to individualism which, in turn, leads to high rates of suicide. The causal links he identifies should, *a fortiori*, be verified for the developed societies of the twentieth century. The twentieth century experienced more growth than the previous century and individualism continued to grow in all sectors of social life. This is the diagnosis made by Norbert Elias, who speaks (1939) of a 'society of individuals'.

All historians who have looked at the material dimensions of civilization have demonstrated that increased material well-being allows individuals to live more independent and autonomous lives. The example of housing exemplifies this trend over hundreds of years.[4] All

---

[4] The collective study published under the general editorship of Philippe Ariès and Georges Duby traces the history of this process of individualization in very concrete terms. See in particular the individual volumes edited by Michelle Perrot (1987) and Antoine Prost (1987).

members of the extended family were once packed into the same shared room (and often the same bed), which was used for all purposes: it was at once a kitchen, a bedroom, a living room and a dining room. The gradual rise in the standard of living led to spatial differentiation, as a distinction came to be made between the kitchen and the dining room, the living room and the bedrooms, and the parents' bedroom and the children's bedrooms. In the richest families, each member of the family eventually came to have their own space and appliances: a bedroom, a television set, a telephone . . . On this uninterrupted march towards ever greater individualism, the upper classes are always several lengths ahead of the less favoured social categories. It is in the upper classes that individualism takes root and develops most rapidly. It is not surprising that the feminist movements that demanded that women should be recognized as individuals in their own right, rather than adjuncts in the service of their families and husbands, first appeared in the developed countries and in the most highly educated strata of the population. These very visible trends in housing can also be seen in many other areas. These are, of course, material trends: the transition from rural to urban life, which is both a cause and an effect of the general growth in wealth, makes individuals less dependent upon the calendar imposed on rural life by the cycle of the seasons, work on the land and markets. Months, weeks and days are now temporal spaces that are less constrained and more open to many different individual interpretations and uses. But there are also non-material trends: the freedom to think and to form one's own opinions about urban existence and life in general increases as the levels of education and school attendance rise. Now it is only when a certain level of wealth has been reached that schools and education can develop and become available to the population as a whole. Unthinking acceptance of the dogmas and beliefs imposed by the Church is no longer automatic. The individualization of attitudes and behaviours therefore goes hand in hand with the increase in wealth, both at the general level of the country and also at the level of families and individuals.

We should therefore expect to see a proportional – and thus terrific – rise in suicide rates in all the developed societies of the twentieth century, particularly when the effects of the continuous and pronounced trend towards individualization can be reinforced by economic crises. Durkheim was convinced that, in the absence of any regulation, the economy of modern societies condemned them to live in a generalized climate of anomie that found periodical expression in economic crises that lead to suicide. And he believed that crises of prosperity seem to be more dangerous than any others. It is not poverty that kills; it is crises themselves, regardless of whether they bring poverty or prosperity (Durkheim 1897: 264): 'So little is it the case that a rise in poverty leads to a rise in suicide that even fortunate crises, the effect of which is rapidly to increase a country's prosperity, act on suicide in the same way as economic disasters.'

If industrial or financial crises do lead to an increase in suicide, it is not because they lead to impoverishment, as 'fortunate crises' have the same effect. They do so because they are crises which disrupt the collective order. Durkheim therefore energetically refutes the hypothesis that economic distress has an aggravating effect on suicide: 'Any disturbance, even when it results in greater wealth and an increase in general vitality, drives some to suicide' (1897: 267). Carried away by his theory of anomie, which ascribes a negative social effect to any weakening or relaxation of the prevailing system of rules, he attributes all crises with the power to overthrow the earlier system of regulation that enabled individuals to control their desires and to restrict their aspirations to levels appropriate to their condition. Discussing the stock market collapse of 1882, the bankruptcy statistics and especially variations in the price index, he concludes (1897: 264) that it is not poverty that kills, as when there is greater prosperity and prices rise, there are more suicides. He notes that there is an increase in suicides in Prussia, if the price of corn either rises or falls.

He goes even further by asserting, in a passage that was to become famous (Durkheim 1897: 267):

> What even better demonstrates that economic hardship does not have the aggravating effect often attributed to it is that it tends rather to produce the opposite. In Ireland [. . .] very few people kill themselves. Poverty-stricken Calabria has virtually no suicides, while Spain has ten times fewer than France. One might even say that poverty protects. In the French provinces, there are more suicides the more people there are of independent means.

When it comes to sudden disturbances of equilibrium, the twentieth century equalled or even surpassed the record of the nineteenth: the crisis of 1929, the *Trente Glorieuses*, the oil crisis. All the conditions existed that should have confirmed Durkheim's prognosis that the twentieth century would see a never ending rise in the number of suicides. Yet that is far from being the case.

3 The Great Turning Point

Despite the alarmist predictions of Durkheim and his Italian prede-
cessor Morselli, the suicide rate did stop rising one day. From 1910 or
1920 onwards, depending on which country we are talking about,
national suicide rates ceased to rise and even began to fall in most
European countries. In 1975, the suicide rate was below that for 1900
in Italy, Great Britain and France. In Austria, it peaked in 1925 and
then began to decline. In Sweden and Denmark, the number of suicides remained stable between 1900 and 1950, after having begun to
decline before 1900. What is more important is that the contrast in the
situation between the developed regions and the rest tended to be
reversed in all countries. In the nineteenth century suicide was an
urban phenomenon; rates are now lowest in metropolitan cities such
as London, Paris and New York. It is as though the twentieth century
had developed new ways of protecting individuals. The nineteenth
century therefore begins to look like a phase in a revolution in social
behaviours that had yet to be accompanied by a corresponding 'civilizing of manners'. After having overturned the old ways of life,
modern urban and industrial society seems to have established new
ones which are not so directly perceptible. Declining suicide rates are,
however, testimony to the fact that they are real. It is in fact as if the
most highly developed societies have found a way of reducing the perverse effects that they initially generated. Where suicide is concerned,
at least.

Let us take a careful look at Fig. 3.1 (page 38), which traces the evolution of suicide rates in France and Great Britain in the nineteenth
and twentieth centuries.

The differences are blindingly obvious: the British rate is always
lower and its variations fluctuate within narrower limits. The French
rate went from a low of 5 per 100,000 at the beginning of this period
to a peak of 25 at the end of the nineteenth century and the beginning

Figure 3.1 Evolution of suicide in Great Britain and France, 19th and 20th centuries (men and women)

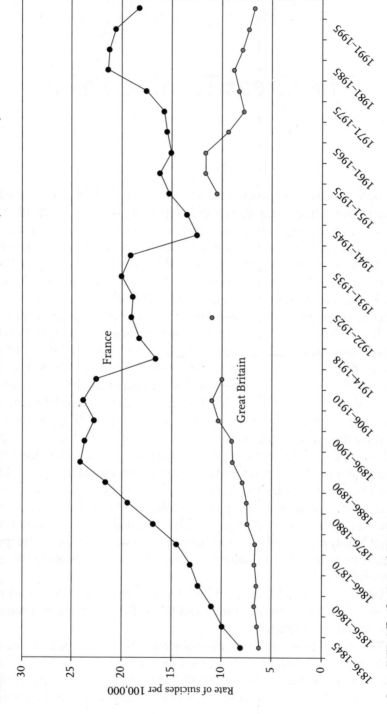

Source: INED Office for National Statistics.

of the twentieth. The British rate remained steadily within the range of between 6 and 12 per 100,000. The average French rate was therefore higher and subject to greater variations than the British rate. At the end of the twentieth century, the curves begin to diverge; suicide rates began to rise again in the 1970s in France at a time when they were falling on the other side of the Channel.

Yet despite these differences, which we will consider later, it is obvious that there are great similarities in the overall profile. In both cases, the trend rises throughout the nineteenth century and displays a more or less pronounced tendency to fall or to stabilize in the twentieth.

Direct comparisons of suicide rates at the beginning and end of the twentieth century reveal a decline in all European countries. This fall is, however, greatly underestimated because the population of Europe as a whole is ageing. In the nineteenth century, as in the twentieth, the suicide rate rises with age. The ageing of the population there tends automatically to raise the unadjusted suicide rate. To take the example of France for the century 1901–2001: the suicide rate falls from 22.6 per 100,000 to 17.6. That the rate fell is beyond dispute. If France had had the same age profile in 2001 as in 1901, its suicide rate would have been 14.4 per 100,000. Which means that suicide rates by average age fell considerably. As the ageing of the population is an attested fact in all rich countries, the trend identified in France applies to all countries.

Because they were firmly rooted in the nineteenth century, the founding fathers of the sociology of suicide – Morselli in Italy and Durkheim in France – ruled out that hypothesis. They were both convinced that the advent of a modern society based on the autonomy of individuals would inevitably lead to a rise in the number of suicides.

'England brings us a surprise!'

Maurice Halbwachs was the first to challenge these prophets of doom. In 1930, he argued (Halbwachs 1930: 64) that: 'It is [. . .] not demonstrated, as is sometimes believed, that the proportion of suicides increases in a continuous and unlimited manner.' As he had access to longer temporal series than Durkheim and Morselli and paid close attention to the inflexions of the curves and to the distribution of the phenomenon around average values, he demonstrated that between 1830 and 1913, the suicide rate was already beginning to decline in two European countries, namely Norway and Denmark. His full attention was drawn to the case of Denmark. In the 1880s, Denmark, which Morselli called 'the homeland of Hamlet, the classic suicidal country' (cited in Halbwachs 1930: 65), was the country with the highest number of suicides. Three historic peaks were reached between 1856 and 1880: 28.4, 27.7 and 26.7 per 100,000, which meant that Denmark's suicide rate was two and a half times higher than the general average for the eleven European countries with the highest number of suicides. And then, against all expectations, the suicide rate on the terraces of Ellsinore fell continuously from 1876–1880 onwards. In 1926, Halbwachs's final observation was that it had fallen by half compared with its peaks, down to Swedish levels. Denmark was the first country to record a spectacular fall in its suicide rates after having had some of the highest.

Far from being an isolated case, this was part of a trend that was to become more common in the twentieth century. Maurice Halbwachs succeeded in identifying it on the basis of very discrete indices at the moment when it was just beginning to take off. Examining in great detail changes in the suicide rates for various regions of France, Italy, Germany and England, Maurice Halbwachs was struck by the transformations in the geography of suicide in all four countries. The growth of the phenomenon was slowing down in those regions where rates were highest, and accelerating in those where they were lowest. In France, the rate was slowing down in the north and rising in the centre. It was increasing in Prussia, but declining in Saxony. It was slackening off around London, Manchester and Liverpool, and rising in Wales, which had previously been spared. There was a link between these contradictory trends and the population movements that were moving a growing mass of individuals from the countryside into the big cities. Between 1880 and 1914 in France and Germany, and especially Great Britain, suicide rates were rising faster in regions where the population was in decline, and rising more slowly in those regions were the population was growing, in other words, in the big industrial conurbations. The big cities were still spreading their tentacles, but their pressure was suffocating fewer individuals.

The observant Halbwachs was beginning to detect a completely new link between suicide and development. At the turn of the century in France, as in Great Britain, but also in Germany and Italy, the great concentrations of people brought together in urban centres and industrial cities were gradually becoming less of a threat to deracinated individuals. The new poles of economic development were becoming the new centres of social life: 'Small cities and peasant groups, in departments which are losing population, are losing a very large part of their resources [. . .] traditions are being disturbed there without anything to replace them, and [. . .] their economic life is becoming more difficult, while in departments which are becoming more populous, the standard of living is rising' (Halbwachs 1930: 95). The growth of the urban population, a direct index of economic development, and the social density it generated were becoming factors that discouraged the increase in suicide. And in this area, England, the first home of the industrial revolution was, after Denmark, leading the way. Maurice Halbwachs was not wrong about this change, which prefigured a profound transformation in the link between suicide and economic development: 'England brings us a surprise!' (1930: 102).

The differences between the towns and the countryside were becoming less marked because the towns were tightening their hold on the regions of which they were now the centre (Halbwachs 1930: 125–126):

Large, medium and small cities, and country towns, are now contained in a total system [. . .] The railroads, the mail and telegraph, the telephones, the branch offices of the banks and large stores are not extended from large and medium cities to small localities because the latter have imitated the neighbouring cities and borrowed those institutions from them. They have not imitated; rather they have been assimilated, which is very different.

Subsequent history does not fully confirm the diagnosis of a national homogenization of suicide rates because, from the 1930s onwards, the gap between towns and the countryside increased again, but this time to the detriment of the latter, which had much higher suicide rates than the urban centres. Let us leave that aside for the moment. The important point is that the suicide curves of the early twentieth century are inverted and that life styles levelled out in the big cities. The emergence of an 'urban civilization' was highly significant in the case of England.

A study by a British historian (Anderson 1987) provides a convergent analysis of the reversal of the trend and goes a long way towards explaining it.

When she analysed the statistics for suicide in her country over the last two centuries and with more particular reference to the Victorian (1837–1901) and Edwardian (1901–1910) periods, Olive Anderson was struck by two facts and related them to one another. On the one hand, the gap between the number of young and old people who committed suicide increased over this period, especially in the big cities and particularly in London, where the contrast was greater than elsewhere: men aged between 55 and 64 committed suicide between ten and twenty times more often than young men. On the other hand, the difference between suicide rates in the big cities and the country-side, which was strongly biased towards the industrial metropolitan areas at the beginning of the period, gradually fell and was then reversed, especially in the case of young men, many fewer of whom killed themselves in the cities than in the countryside.

Suicide amongst girls was less frequent in Edwardian London (between 1901 and 1910) than in the provinces, as was suicide amongst men and women over the age of 65. This reversal upsets the traditional explanation that was in fashion during the Victorian era: suicide was associated with unhealthy sprawling metropolitan areas, which were seen as dens of iniquity. Olive Anderson explains this reversal by demonstrating (1987: 55–56) that the industrial environment in, for example, the textile districts of Lancashire, was better for young people than the old. They found work easily, earned wages that gave them increased purchasing power and, as young workers, enjoyed a social status that gave them a respected place in the society of the day. The new technologies of the industrial economy and the economic boom of the Victorian period worked in favour of young people but penalized older workers who found it more difficult to adapt to the new order.

The big cities were gradually becoming more human and more civ-ilized. Food was better there, and there was more of it. Young children were beginning to attend school. Mortality rates were falling. Olive Anderson suggested that whilst the number of suicides, as a propor-tion of the living (the population as a whole), tended to fall in London, it tended to rise when compared with the total deaths in any given period. Suicide was an increasingly common cause of death because other causes (illness, etc.) were declining in importance and because the population's state of health was improving. Under Edward VII London was the town with the fewest suicides in all England. The gap between young and old was increasing: between 1911 and 1913, a man of 65 was seven times more likely to commit suicide than a girl aged between 15 and 24. The economic boom of the period guaranteed the young working population of London and their families living condi-tions that were incomparably better than those of earlier periods, and the working class was enjoying greater respectability. According to

Olive Anderson (1987: 65), the ten-year reign of Edward VII coincided with 'the advent in big towns and cities of a comparative paradise for young people'. That is why, in her view, we see a fall in suicide rates amongst young people and people living in the big cities between the Victorian period and the Edwardian period. The increasing gap between and men and women over 65 is explained by the devaluation and deskilling of older workers, whose wages were falling, whilst housewives were spared that experience. She adds a further interpretation, which is directly inspired by Durkheim: old women found it easier than old men to find work caring for children or doing housework. Women enjoyed greater support and 'ties of affection were likely to be stronger with mothers than with fathers' (1987: 63) and 'the economic compensations of widowhood were probably greater among the poorer families' (1987: 64). Men who had spent most of their lives out of doors found 'retirement' more difficult because it meant the Work House and being 'confined to two bare rooms and a treeless yard' (1987: 64).

Having disrupted social life for more than one hundred years, the industrial revolution in England was finally providing young people, people living in the towns and workers with greater material and moral resources than the countryside. In the first years of the twentieth century, a new pattern of suicide and new links between suicide and economic development were gradually established in England. This would last until the oil crisis hit the developed countries in the 1970s.

France in the nineteenth and twentieth centuries: the twists and turns in the evolution of suicide

Whilst France did not escape the general trend, it was characterized by specific deviations from the rule. Over the last two hundred years, the curve of the evolution of suicide has been subject to several different trends (see Fig. 3.2 on page 44).

Throughout the nineteenth century, we find that the suicide rate rises rapidly and continuously, except around the time of the war of 1870. It is not irrelevant that Durkheim conceived and wrote his book – which was published in 1897 – at the point when the phenomenon was at its height. The last years of the nineteenth century were characterized by a slight decrease in the phenomenon between 1898 and 1904, and then by an upturn. The suicide rate reached around 25 per 100,000 between 1906 and 1908 and this historic record

Figure 3.2 Evolution of suicide rate in France (1827–2000)

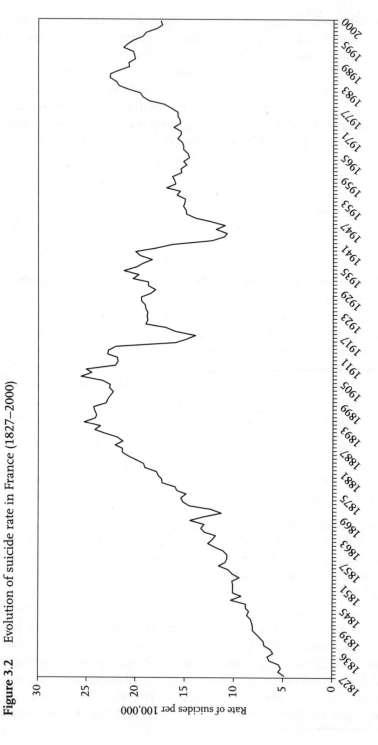

Source: INED.

has never been equalled. The rate came near that level for a very brief period in the late twentieth century, when rates came close to 23 per 100,000 in 1985, 1986 and 1987.

The evolution of the phenomenon was less linear than in the previous century, and has a jagged profile in the twentieth century. From the beginning of the twentieth century until the end of the Second World War, the overall trend was downward and the suicide rate fell from 25 per 100,000 in 1908 to 11.2 in 1946. But far from being continuous, the irregular downward trend was punctuated by sporadic rises. There was a steep fall up until the end of the First World War, followed by a net rise during the years 1920–1930, then a spectacular fall during the Second World War.

After the war, the number of suicides rose slightly before becoming relatively stable during the *Trente Glorieuses* and until the end of the 1970s. During the 1980s, the rise was sharp and rapid; the suicide rate then fell back to levels close to those for the periods immediately before and after the peaks of 1894–1898 and 1906–1908.

How are we to explain these irregular but large-scale variations in the suicide rate over the last two hundred years in the context of the development of the economy? It is all very well to say that the explanatory factors are to be found in the immediate environment of the individuals who commit suicide, and in their family environment in particular, but it is difficult not to try to establish a link between the curve and other trends which express, at the macroscopic level, some of the major transformations French society has experienced over the last hundred years.

One thing is obvious: as Durkheim had already observed, the effect of wars on the fall in the number of suicides is broadly confirmed by the spectacular falls in the suicide rate during the last three 'Great Wars' France experienced in 1870, 1914 and 1940. Durkheim himself observed this phenomenon during the war of 1870 when, in France, Saxony and Prussia, the number of suicides fell significantly between 1869 and 1871. Nothing of the kind happened in 1870 in England, which was spared this conflict: 'Great upheavals in society, like great popular wars, sharpen collective feelings, stimulate the party spirit and the national one and, by concentrating activities towards a single end, achieve, at least for a time, a greater integration of society' (Durkheim 1897: 223).

But when it comes to medium- and long-term developments that cause general social upheavals – outside these periods of war – we have to look at the economic infrastructure if we wish to find

Figure 3.3 Evolution of suicide rate and purchasing power, France, 1900–1998 (suicides per 100 million; purchasing power = average per capita income of 1998 francs)

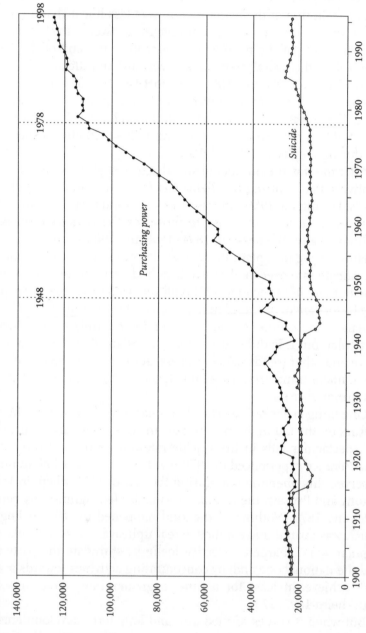

Sources: Suicide, INED; purchasing power, T. Piketty *Les Hauts revenus en France au XXe siècle*, Grasset, 2001.

indicators relating to material conditions of existence, living standards, and to the sum total and distribution of disposable wealth.

As we have seen, Émile Durkheim took the view that crises are the main factor explaining the link between suicide and economic growth. Thirty years later, Maurice Halbwachs criticized the indicators used by Durkheim, and particularly the price index, which do not take into account financial crises. He also stressed that it is very difficult to pinpoint the specific impact that the economy has on suicide. Basing his argument on Germany during the post-1880 economic boom (1880–1913) and, to a lesser extent, on France, he demonstrates that the relationship between suicide and prices is not the same in the two countries. In Germany, the phenomenon is clear. The number of suicides falls when prices rise, and rises when prices fall. The trend is less obvious in France, where suicide rates can also rise when prices fall. What is more important, Halbwachs criticizes (1930: 743–744) the very principle behind Durkheim's analysis, which sees crises as the main or sole explanatory factor:

> Not the crisis as such [. . .] but the period of depression following the crisis is what causes an increase in voluntary deaths [. . .] The woes of unemployed workers, the bankruptcies, failures and downfalls are not the immediate cause of many suicides. Rather, an obscure oppressive sentiment weighs on every soul because there is less general activity, because there is less participation by people in an economic life transcending them, and because their attention is no longer turned towards externals but dwells more, not merely on their distress or on their bare material competency, but on all the individual motives they may have for desiring death.

It is not, according to Halbwachs, only the rich who suffer so badly during economic crises that they take their own lives.

Thomas Piketty (2001: 70f and appendices) has reconstructed, on the basis of fiscal data, series of high-quality economic indicators for the whole of the twentieth century: purchasing power measured by average per capita income, average household income, share of distributed income monopolized by the richest households, average general wages, consumer price indices, etc. These indicators, which are much more direct than the GDP series, are well suited to our purposes.

The series constructed by Piketty reveal a 'dizzying rise in purchasing power' throughout the twentieth century: average per capita income (in 1998 francs) rose 6.5 times between 1900 and 1998. Household income rose 4.5 times. At the beginning of the twentieth century, the average household had an income equivalent to the 1998

RMI [*Revenu Minimum d'Insertion*], whereas the income of the average household was four and a half times higher at the end of the century, even though households were smaller.

The rate at which purchasing power rose (an average of 1.54 per annum) was not, however, constant. It varied from period to period, and in line with GDP. The profile of the overall curve allows Piketty to identify three main stages in the growth of the average income, or in other words of the French standard of living from 1900 to 1998.

The first period (1900–1948) coincides with the first half of the century. It is characterized by the near-stagnation of average income, with average per capita income enjoying a growth rate of 0.42.

During the second period of prosperity, or the three decades after the Second World War (1948–1978), average per capita income experienced an exceptional rate of growth: 5.0.

The third period (1978–1998) is characterized by a sharp downturn in growth from the mid-1970s onwards. The growth rate of average per capita income fell to 1.22.

If we correlate the curves for purchasing power and suicide rates over these three major periods, and look both at the profile of the curves and the coefficient of correlation, several conclusions emerge.

The years in which suicide rates were at their highest occur at the dawn and dusk of the twentieth century: the two peaks when the suicide rate comes close to or exceeds 25 per 100,000 – 1906, 1907, 1908, and 1985, 1986 and 1987 – occur in very different economic contexts: purchasing power was at its lowest and its highest in the twentieth century, irrespective of whether it is measured in terms of GDP or average income. In the twentieth century, suicide rates peaked at similar levels when the French were poorest and richest, with a wage earner's purchasing power (in 1998 francs) of 25,000 francs at the beginning of the century, and 120,000 at the end. There is therefore no direct link between suicide and absolute purchasing power.

The lowest suicide rates (between 10 and 15 per 100,000) basically coincide with years of war or the immediate post-war years: 1916 and 1917, and 1942, 1943, 1944, 1945, 1947 and 1948. Both suicide rates and purchasing power fell spectacularly during both the First and Second World Wars. The war of 1940 caused purchasing power to plummet to its lowest level; it had the same effect on the suicide rate, which reached it lowest point of the century in 1943 and 1944 (11 per 100,000). The fall in the suicide rate and in purchasing power went hand in hand: the war appears to have a greater effect than purchasing power.

Table 3.1   Relationship between suicide and purchasing power, 1900–1998

1900–1948		1949–1978		1979–1998	
Purchasing power	Suicide	Purchasing power	Suicide	Purchasing power	Suicide
=	−	+	=	−	+

The link between suicide and purchasing power during the three significant periods identified by Thomas Piketty is equally instructive. Taking the period as a whole, there is little correlation between the two evolutions (0.19). If we replace changes in purchasing power with GDP, the link is similar and on the same scale. The link between suicide rates and the increase in wealth is not identifiable at first sight, even though the profile of the curves seems to indicate that the rhythms of economic life and those of the suicide rate are related, even though they are not quite synchronous.

The three periods are characterized by different links between purchasing power and the suicide rate:

1900–1948 was a period of upheavals but, on the whole, purchasing power remained almost stable, whilst the suicide rate tended to fall. Negative correlation: −0.33.

1949–1978: dizzying rise in purchasing power, stagnation of suicide rate. A positive but weak correlation: 0.14.

1979–1995: growth slows down, but per capita purchasing power rises very slightly (at the same time domestic purchasing power falls: −0.01). Big rise in the suicide rate. Strong positive correlation: 0. 62.

The interesting thing about this one-hundred-year temporal series is that it reveals different instances of the relationship between suicide and purchasing power. When purchasing power remains stable, the number of suicides falls; suicides also remain stable when purchasing power increases sharply and rapidly; they rise when purchasing power declines. It is still difficult to draw any firm conclusions from these findings, except to note that twentieth-century France does not confirm Durkheim's peremptory assertion that 'poverty protects'. If crises of prosperity did increase the risk of suicide, there would have been a big rise in the number of suicides during the *Trente Glorieuses*, and then a decrease. We find precisely the opposite. The near stability of the suicide rate over thirty years of strong growth also refutes the conclusions drawn from the synchronic relationship between GDP and the suicide rate at the international level (the richer the country, the higher its suicide rate . . .).

Figure 3.4 Evolution of suicide rate and purchasing power, France, 1900–1948 (suicides per 100 million; purchasing power = average per capita income of 1998 francs)

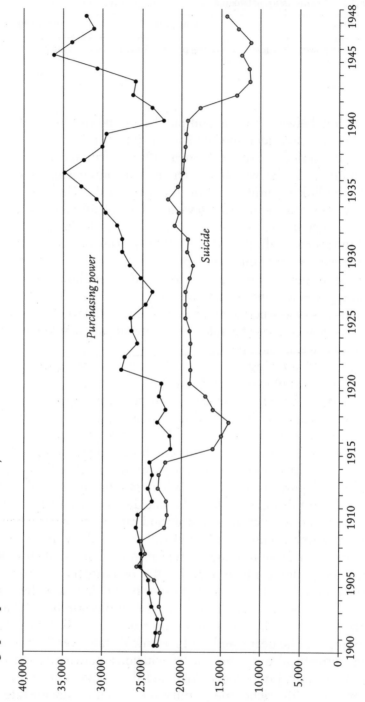

Sources: Suicide, INED; purchasing power, T. Piketty *Les Hauts revenus en France au XXe siècle,* Grasset, 2001.

In twentieth-century France, it is the increase in purchasing power that protects against suicide, the suicide rate rising when it slows down. The fact that purchasing power was stable during the first half of the century is an expression of an average but very uneven trend. We should therefore look more closely at the facts and examine in detail the meandering curves for each of the three periods of economic development.

1900–1948: the parallel between suicide and growth breaks down

This period is certainly the most problematic: it is the longest, the most disrupted in economic terms and the most heterogeneous in social and political terms (two world wars, an economic depression, the Popular Front . . .). For our purposes, it is also the most interesting because, being characterized as a whole by a negative correlation between suicide and purchasing power, it reveals different instances of the relationship between the two. When averaged out, purchasing power falls over this period, but its overall decline is neither constant nor continuous. Although purchasing power has its highs and lows, the curve is broken and unsteady (see Fig. 3.4 on page 50).

The explanation for the chaotic evolution of purchasing power is the repeated turbulence caused by the two world wars and the economic crisis of the 1930s. Between 1900 and 1914, there was a slight rise in average household income. The downturn in production during the war years caused it to fall. The reconstruction and strong growth of the 1920s resulted in an almost 15% rise in purchasing power as compared with the pre-war period. The return of inflation in 1926 and stabilization under the Poincaré government led to a new fall in purchasing power, which fell back to its pre-war level. The economy began to grow again in 1928–1930, but by 1931, the economic crisis led to new falls in purchasing power, even though the 1930s were characterized by the stagnation of purchasing power rather than by an actual decline. 'The Second World War and the downturn in production that went with it causes the purchasing power of the average income to fall to the lowest level recorded in France during the twentieth century' (Piketty 2001). At the end of the Second World War, average household income (in 1998 francs) was at a very similar level to what it was before the First World War. It was only in 1945–46 that it returned to the level it had been before the Second World War, and only in 1948–49 that it finally rose above that level. The jagged profile of the evolution of purchasing power, whose causes are well known,

Table 3.2   Coefficients of correlation between suicide and purchasing power in the same year and put back a year

	1900–1913	1914–1919	1919–1925	1926–1930	1931–1939	1940–1948
Suicide and purchasing power (same year)	0.39	0.67	−0.05	−0.05	0.06	−0.68
Suicide and purchasing power (year N+1)	**0.60**	0.22	**0.93**	**−0.93**	**0.60**	**−8.5**

suggests that we have to look closely at how it relates to the suicide rate in each sub-period.

1900–1913: purchasing power rises slightly; the suicide rate rises and then falls.

1914–1918: purchasing power falls, as does the suicide rate.

1919–1925: purchasing power rises, and the suicide rate is stable.

1926–1930: purchasing power rises, and the suicide rate is stable.

1931–1939: purchasing power rises slightly and the suicide rate is stable.

1940–1948: purchasing power falls and then recovers; the suicide rate falls.

The two wars, during which the suicide rate fell and purchasing power declined, are the sole causes of the sharp fall in the suicide rate in the first half of the twentieth century: the post-war rate never returns to its pre-war level. It is during these periods that we find the closest correlation between the two magnitudes, and war obviously has a greater effect than purchasing power. Outside these very distinctive periods, peacetime seems to promote a happier relationship between suicide and purchasing power. The suicide rate remains stable or falls when purchasing power rises. Wealth therefore appears to have a beneficial effect. It appears to prevent the suicide rate from rising and sometimes causes it to fall. This relationship is new, as the situation was the reverse during the nineteenth century, when the suicide rate rose as the nation's wealth increased.

These trends become more pronounced if, instead of establishing the coefficient of correlation between the two magnitudes for the same year, we put back the suicide rate temporal series by a year. We can then measure the effect of the conjunctural rise or fall in purchasing power on the morale and behaviour of individuals in the following year. This presumes that the economic situation has a delayed effect on the suicide rate rather than an instantaneous effect, a hypothesis that is more in keeping with reality. Changing the system of measurement does not alter the trend we are observing, but it does accentuate it by establishing a much closer link between the two phenomena: suicide rate and purchasing power.

The correlation recorded between purchasing power and the suicide rate over the period as a whole (-0.33 if the two phenomena are measured in the same year, and -0.37 if the suicide rate is backdated by a year) is softened by the broken line and the ups and downs in the rise and fall of purchasing power. When we correlate the suicide rate and purchasing power over shorter and economically homogenous economic periods – in which the trend may be upward, downward or stable – relations between the suicide rate and purchasing power become clearer and move in the opposite direction to that ascribed to them by Durkheim. What happens in the other two periods?

1949–1978: strong growth, stable suicide rates

The relationship between the suicide rate and purchasing power is much clearer and moves lineally throughout this period of high growth, but it also confirms the trend recorded in the previous period: a dizzying rise in purchasing power accompanies a stable suicide rate see (Fig. 3.5 on page 54).

We therefore have to think again about the social effects of this period of growth. Durkheim's intuition is refuted, and Halbwachs's observations about Germany at the end of the nineteenth century are confirmed. The number of suicides did not decline but remained stable, hovering around an average level of 15 per 100,000, or in other words a low level that had not, with the exception of periods of war, been seen in France since the end of the 1870s. This stagnation at a low level (for France . . .) after the turbulent inter-war period represents a spectacular transformation and it is difficult not to link it to the very special features of the economic situation. Purchasing power more than quadrupled in thirty years.

With the exception of the short period of a return of inflation around 1958, which was accompanied by a slight but definite rise in suicide rates,[1] there was a steady annual increase in purchasing power over a

[1] The rate rose to 17.3, 16.4, 16.5, and 16.7 in 1957, 1958, 1959 and 1960, respectively. After 1960, it fell to its pre-1957 rate of about 15 per 100,000. This confirms that the suicide rate is very sensitive to the fluctuations of economic life.

Figure 3.5 Evolution of suicide rate and purchasing power, France, 1949–1978 (suicides per 100 million; purchasing power = average per capita income of 1998 francs)

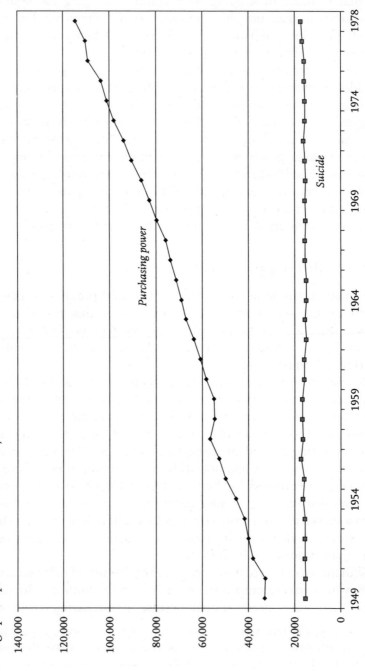

Sources: Suicide, INED; purchasing power, T. Piketty *Les Hauts revenus en France au XXe siècle*, Grasset, 2001.

period of thirty years. The situation of growth typical of the *Trente Glorieuses* certainly generated many factors encouraging welfare and the possibility of planning for the future. This was true for individuals (full employment, a rising standard of living, a higher percentage of children in full-time education, careers and promotion) households (fertility, access to property), and society as a whole (social security, planning, the Common Programme of the Left, and the various social projects drawn up by parties, associations and political groups, social struggles . . .). All these conditions protect individuals from suicide.

1979–1995: slower growth, more suicides

Things are very different in the following period, which was characterized by a downturn in growth and purchasing power and by a steep rise in the suicide rate, which rises from about 15 per 100,000 in the mid-1970s to over 23 in 1985, with a historic peak being recorded in 1986 (26 per 100,000). As for purchasing power, 'the rising trend seems to have been completely reversed [. . .] That the standard of living rose more slowly than in the earlier period is quite true, which explains why it had such a large negative impact [. . .] Average per capita income, which grew at an annual rate of 5% between 1948 and 1998, fell to 1.2%, or to a level four times lower than that of the earlier period' (Piketty 2001: 75) (see Fig. 3.6 on page 56).

The coefficient of correlation between the suicide rate and purchasing power is positive and very high (0.62, which is the highest correlation observed for the whole century; it reaches 0.68 if we move the temporal series of suicide rates back by one year). Purchasing power rises from 100 to 111, and the suicide rate from 100 to 127. The two therefore rise in parallel, but with one difference: purchasing power experiences a slow but constant increase, whereas suicide rates begin by rising, peak in 1986 and then decline, returning in 1995 to the 1990 level. The rise in the suicide rate appears to be bound up with the downturn in the growth of purchasing power, with a break in the rhythm rather than with the direction of the trend. How else can we explain the peak and then the break in 1985–1987? Why the peak and why the downward trend, when there is no break in the slow increase in purchasing power?

It is difficult not to make a connection between the sharp increase in the suicide rate during this period and the new social climate generated in France by the transformations of economic life resulting from the oil crises in the mid-1970s. The late 1970s saw the beginning of a new economic period that challenged many of the welfare and

Figure 3.6   Evolution of suicide rate and purchasing power, France, 1979–
1995 (suicide per 100 million; purchasing power = average per capita
income of 1998 francs)

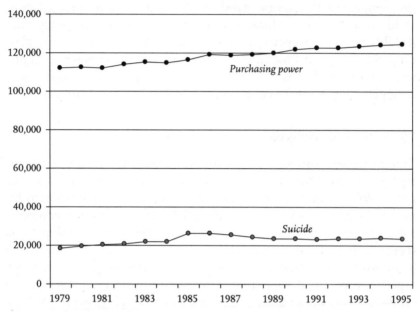

Sources: Suicide, INED; purchasing power, T. Piketty *Les Hauts revenus en France au XXe siècle,*
Grasset, 2001.

social security measures workers had enjoyed during the thirty years
of growth. The appearance of a high level of long-term mass unemployment was certainly one of the period's most conspicuous features.
Against a background of unemployment, the main factors in economic life were thrown into turmoil. International competition and
the globalization of markets led companies to adapt to the new situation: the closure or relocation of firms and huge waves of redundan-
cies on the one hand, the intensification of work, an end to job security
and the increasing flexibility of working rhythms on the other. On top
of all that, the imperatives of finance capital and stock-market specu-
lation became more dictatorial. It was at this time that the theme of
exclusion made its appearance and met with growing popularity in
those circles responsible for the analysis and management of the negative effects of the new economic situation: sociologists, economists,
social workers, trade unionists, government advisers and politicians.
This was also the moment when, as a result of the liberal measures
taken by government of both the left and the right, the cement that
protected and integrated a wage-based society began to crack and

disintegrate. Robert Castel has analysed (1995) in detail the stages of gradual disintegration of this social model. In short, the effect of all these sweeping transformations of economic and social life was to increase insecurity and the feeling of insecurity. A new world was coming into being, and it brought with it a heightened feeling of uncertainty. The spectacular increase in the suicide rate was in any case an indication of the anxiety and insecurity that the new direction of economic and social life engendered. There was another unmistakeable sign. Inequalities had been steadily reduced throughout the twentieth century. After the oil crisis, this trend slowed. The correlation between the rising suicide rate and this indicator of inequality (as defined by the share of taxable income monopolized by the richest 10%) became close and positive in this last period.

It transpires from this re-examination of the French statistics that, outside periods of war, there is a clear link between suicide and purchasing power. First of all, the link is there: the high coefficients of correlation in all the sub-periods clearly testify to the fact that suicide rates are very sensitive to fluctuations in economic life and purchasing power. In the twentieth century, the suicide rate fell or stagnated when purchasing power increased. It rose when purchasing power declined or slowed down.

Classic evolution in England

The quality of the available statistics for Great Britain is inferior to that of the French data: the evolution of the yearly suicide rate is available only from 1950 onwards. We are forced to fall back on five- or ten-year aggregates for the period from the beginning of the nineteenth century until 1925. There are no statistics for the period 1925–1950, and the figures we have found are not easily reconciled with those for later years. The wealth indicator used derives from Angus Maddison's reconstructions of GDP (Maddison 2001). Whilst these series are respectable, they do not come near the quality of the homogeneous series for purchasing power established for the whole of the nineteenth century by Thomas Piketty. Figure 3.7 therefore suffers from some obvious approximations.

One trend does, however, stand out clearly. Whereas suicide rates and economic growth were parallel in the nineteenth century and up to 1925 – the suicide rate rose as the country became wealthier – the relationship between the two was then reversed. From 1925 onwards, the suicide rate fell as Great Britain became more affluent.

Figure 3.7 Evolution of suicide rates and GDP, Great Britain, 1820–2000

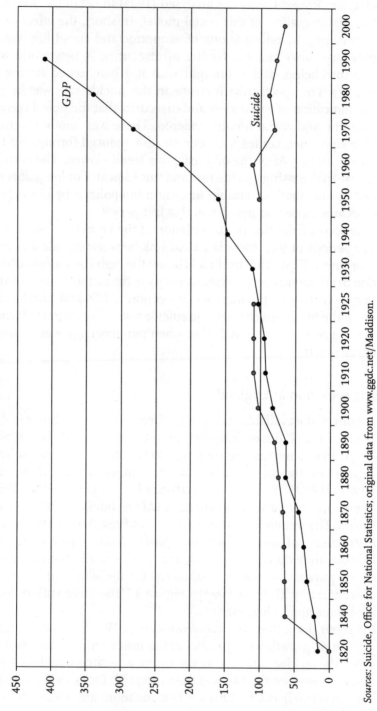

Sources: Suicide, Office for National Statistics; original data from www.ggdc.net/Maddison.

Figure 3.8 Evolution of suicide rates and GDP, Great Britain 1950–2000

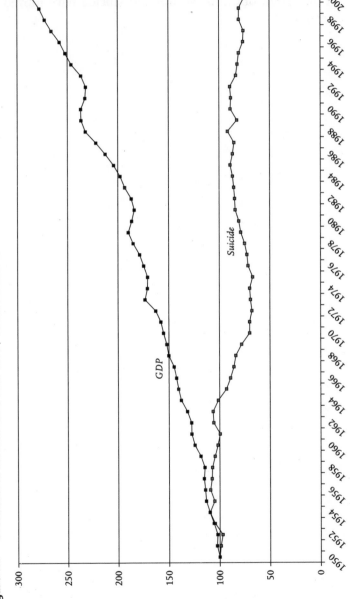

Sources: Suicide, Office for National Statistics; original data from www.ggdc.net/Maddison.

The phenomenon became particular apparent in the second half of the twentieth century (Fig. 3.8 on page 59).

This was a period of uninterrupted growth in Great Britain: after stabilizing slightly in the 1950s, the suicide rate clearly fell but, unlike the French rate, showed no particular inflexions at the time of the oil crisis. From that point onwards, wealth and suicide have moved in different directions.

4 The *Trente Glorieuses*

Between 1945 and 1975, the wealth of most industrialized countries increased at an unprecedented rate. In the space of thirty years, per capita wealth doubled in Australia, New Zealand, Canada, Switzerland, Sweden and Denmark, tripled in Belgium, Finland, Germany and France, quintupled in Italy and the Netherlands, and increased eightfold in Japan. In 1975, all these nations caught up with the hitherto fabled level of the United States: before the war, its level of affluence had been three to four times greater than theirs, but by 1975 it was only one third higher.

Now, in what looks in retrospect like a blessed period in terms of dynamic growth, we do not find the continuous and general rise in the suicide rate that might have been extrapolated from the data for the nineteenth century. Between 1950 and 1975, the suicide rate remained practically unchanged in Australia, Austria, Belgium, Denmark, Ireland, France and Norway. It rose very slowly in Sweden, the Netherlands and the United States. It fell slightly in Italy, and sharply in Japan and Great Britain. Finland was the only rich country to experience a big rise in the suicide rate: from 15.5 to 25.0 per 100,000 inhabitants.

It is true that these ceilings and even these falls were recorded when the rates were fairly high. When we compare all countries in any given year, their suicide rates are clearly associated with their level of affluence: suicide rates were definitely higher in the richer countries. But in those rich countries, suicide rates and levels of wealth did not rise at the same rate as they had done one hundred years earlier.

State-orchestrated growth

The nineteenth century was characterized by the sudden appearance of new forms of production and social life within a world of old traditions and local customs. The rapid development of the post-war years was, to a large extent, concerted and sometimes even planned. State intervention to organize infrastructure and to stimulate the growth of new branches was common everywhere. The ideas of John Maynard Keynes became state doctrine. One of the key objectives, which was almost completely achieved in this period, was full employment. Public resources were concentrated on this objective, as Keynes had demonstrated that it did not automatically follow on from the equilibrium of the market. In France, the rate of growth and the level of employment were main priorities for four successive economic programmes. The provisions of the Welfare State were part of this framework. By guaranteeing all actors protection against certain accidental mishaps, it allowed them to play a positive role in growth: some of the resources of even the most modest households could be channelled into the acquisition of consumer durables and home-ownership. The American model of the Ford worker became widespread: the worker was both a productive force and one of modern industry's customers, and therefore an essential agent of overall demand. The spectre of a crisis seemed at last to have been exorcized: in the 1960s, Valéry Giscard d'Estaing could guarantee that, thanks to the effects of indicative planning and moderate inflation, economic crises could definitely be ruled out. For most social categories, economic growth was part of the foreseeable future and it allowed them to develop strategies. Surveys of families showed that, convinced that their children would have a better start in life than they had had, parents tried to ensure that the material and symbolic help they gave them helped them achieve that goal. Those social categories that were threatened by these developments, in either the short or the long term, were able to implement retraining strategies, organize themselves into pressure groups and make the authorities bear the cost of some of the upheavals to come. Predictability was an essential part of the process during the *Trente Glorieuses*. When miracles did occur, as they did in Italy, they had always been predicted in advance. The final essential feature of this uninterrupted growth was that it occurred mainly within nation states. The centuries-long construction of a community of citizens transforms individuals into real social actors. And when the State becomes a major economic power, it becomes possible for citizens to influence the development of the economic world in either real or imaginary terms. It seems that inflexible laws are a thing of the past: because they can fight, either individually or collectively, to ensure that the government channels its investments in the right direction, citizens feel that the changes they want are possible and depend upon political decision-making. The economy is not subject only to the inflexible laws of the market. Durkheim's idea that the economy is the victim of a situation of generalized anomie reflects both the brutality of the sudden appearance of capitalism and an ignorance of the major social agents. The State had, until then, been reduced to managing its most brutal and direct effects in an anarchic and vote-seeking fashion: regulating the setting up of department stores, freezing rents, raising customs duties . . . A better understanding of economics and statistics made it possible to take intellectual control of the market economy. Growth therefore occurred in a social context that was very different to that of the nineteenth century. In the nineteenth century, the upheaval in social structures meant that all aspects of growth were associated with a rising suicide rate. The same was not true of the second half of the twentieth century. We can even advance the hypothesis that certain developments associated with the growth of wealth encourage suicide, whilst others discourage it. Let us try to identify some of them.

Aggravating factors . . .

As a country becomes more affluent, individuals take advantage of the margin of freedom granted them by their material affluence in order to take more control over their own lives. They try to free themselves from the collective shackles placed on them by a state of poverty in order to gain more control over their fate: they place their trust in reason rather than religion, are prepared to share their lives only with partners with whom they get along, reduce the size of their families by having only the number of children they want, and take advantage of improved working conditions and advances in medicine in order to live longer. These are the direct effects of the general increase in wealth on the behaviour of individuals. They can be observed in all known societies once a certain level of economic development has been reached. Norbert Elias has demonstrated (1939) that the trend towards the individualization of behaviours is closely associated with what he calls the 'civilizing process'.

Durkheim's sociology of suicide clearly demonstrates that, in the nineteenth century, falling fertility rates, the increase in divorce, the ageing of the population and the decline of religious practice – all forces unleashed as societies became more affluent – were factors that encouraged suicide. Is that still true today, now that, far from loosening their grip, these forces have become widespread and are continuously affecting a growing number of individuals all over the world? Yes and no. Yes, because, taken one at a time, each of these trends is still a factor that increases suicide. No, because, in the second part of the twentieth century, they appear to be cancelled out by the other effects, direct and indirect, of the increase in wealth, which, in contrast, protect individuals from suicide.

All developments that weaken traditional family bonds encourage suicide. That is the most reliable finding of Durkheim's statistics on marital status. Marriage and the number of children individuals have do protect them from suicide. Whilst developments between 1950 and 1975 did not destroy the family, they did transform the appearance of the institution, but without taking away its protective role.

After a rise related to the end of the war, fertility rates fell in all the industrialized countries. And the link between suicide and fertility is well established, as can be seen from Fig. 4.1 (page 65) for the year 1975.

The link between fertility and suicide is highly significant. Given an equal level of GDP, it stays very constant. The more children they have, the less likely people are to commit suicide. Fig. 4.1 again reveals the cumulonimbus hovering over the countries of the Soviet bloc. These countries seem to have been affected by two suicidogenic factors: a low level of fertility and a relatively low GDP. We find that rich countries – Great Britain, the Netherlands, Norway, the United States and Japan – that have low levels of fertility compared with those of countries in the East (1.5 children per woman) have much lower suicide rates. The demographic effects of the growth in wealth constitute risk factors, but wealth in itself appears to provide adequate protection. In the twentieth century, there is no longer a direct link between wealth and suicide.

Having said that, the effects of the growth in wealth are not confined to fertility. The trend towards social relations in which the initiatives and interests of the individual outweigh those of the group – and this is a very long-term trend in Western societies – also tends to weaken family structures as divorce becomes more common. Now the link between divorce and suicide (Fig. 4.2, page 66), which was well established in the nineteenth century, continues to exist in the twentieth, given a constant level of wealth. The link is very strong, as the link between the two phenomena was as strong in 1995 as it was one hundred years earlier. But as the countries of the socialist bloc once more demonstrate, it is not wealth itself that has a direct effect on the

Figure 4.1 Fertility and male suicide in 1975 (rates of male suicide per 100,000)

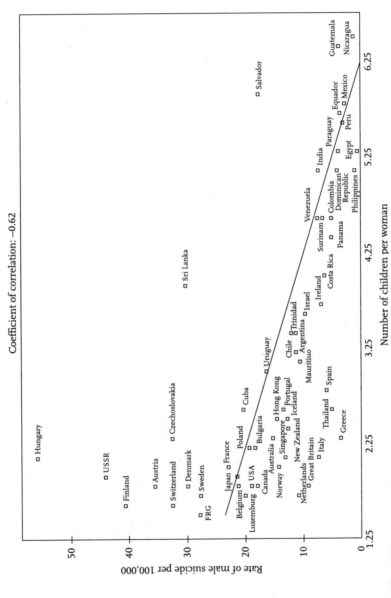

Coefficient of correlation: –0.62

Number of children per woman

Rate of male suicide per 100,000

Source: UNDP, 2002.

Figure 4.2 Divorce and male suicide in 1975 (rates of male suicide per 100,000)

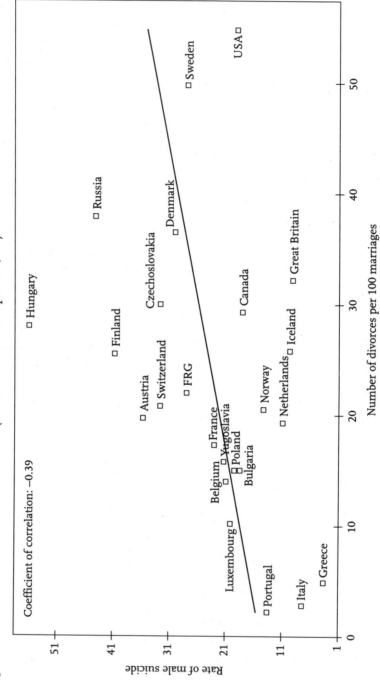

Source: J.-P. Sardon, INED, *Population*, 2004.

suicide rate. Even when it is associated with a small increase in wealth, the frequency of divorce goes hand in hand with very high suicide rates.

Economic growth has, finally, an almost automatic effect on one of the variables most closely associated with suicide: the age of the population. With the exceptions and recent changes we will consider later, suicide rates rise steeply as the age of the population increases in almost all countries and almost all periods. Economic growth increases the marginal cost of a child, so tends to reduce the number of children per household. Developments in medicine provide more effective forms of treatment, whilst improved living conditions and the introduction of major social welfare schemes increase life expectancy. The population thus ages as a result of what is happening at both ends: fewer young people, more old people. In Italy, for instance, the male population aged between 14 and 25 fell from 35% to 32%. That change alone was responsible for 247 more suicides per year (1 in 100,000). That is a high figure because, after a steady rise over that twenty-year period, the suicide rate for Italian men stabilized at 10.1 per 100,000. The ageing of the Italian population accelerated again between 1980 and 2000, the proportion of 14 to 25-year-olds fell to 22% of the population and the proportion of men over 65 rose to 15%. This is a general mechanism that applies to all rich countries. Assuming that the effects of growth are restricted to the transformation of the age pyramid, we should have seen a sustained and continuous rise in suicide rates in all rich countries. That is far from being the case. Growth therefore does have protective effects that are still to be identified. But let us continue with our examination of the aggravating factors.

Regular religious observance discourages suicide. Durkheim and other sociologists of his day placed great emphasis on the protective role of religion in the nineteenth century. Contemporary electoral polls allow the development of religious observance in France to be evaluated with some accuracy. On the eve of the 2005 vote on the European constitution, practising Catholics had been reduced to a minority: 7% according to the Catholic paper *La Croix*. That proportion has fallen steadily since the end of the war, and we can assume that it will continue to fall, as the trend is associated mainly with the replacement of one generation by the next. This phenomenon is very widespread, as we can see from the very close correlation between countries' wealth and their levels of religious observance (Fig. 4.3, page 68). The richer the country, the fewer regular worshippers there are.

Figure 4.3 Wealth and religious observance in 1995

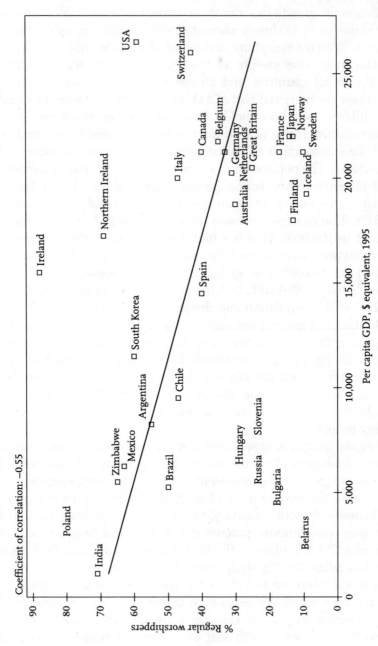

Coefficient of correlation: −0.55

Source: R. Inglehart, *World Values Surveys*, 1995 and 1999.

Figure 4.4 Religion and male suicides in 1995

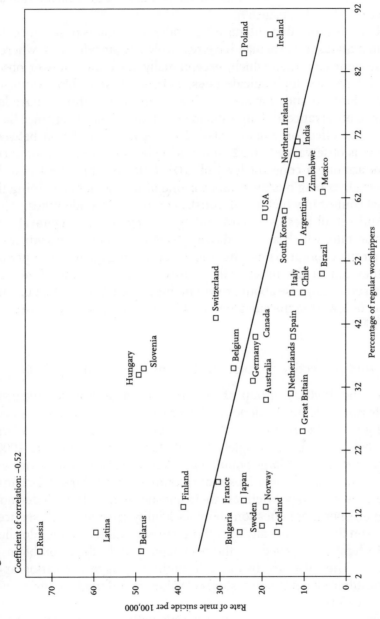

Coefficient of correlation: −0.52

Rate of male suicide per 100,000

Percentage of regular worshippers

Source: R. Inglehart, *World Values Surveys*, 1995 and 1999.

This is a clear trend even though, once again, the paradoxical situation in the countries of the former Soviet bloc attenuates it somewhat. And the effects of religious observance on the suicide rate are still clear (Fig. 4.4, page 69).

Rich countries that still have high rates of religious observance, the United States in particular, have relatively low suicide rates, whereas those poor countries which, exceptionally, have low rates of observance have very high suicide rates, as in the Eastern bloc countries. Japan, Finland and Norway, which are very rich countries, have low rates of observance and high suicide rates. Religious observance has a particular effect on suicide rates. The negative correlation between religious observance (-0.52) and suicide becomes more pronounced if we assume a constant level of GDP (-0.55). This effect is to be expected, as religious observance is one of the elements defining the social context in which we all construct our personal identities.

And yet all these standard and age-old factors that aggravate the suicide rate, which are the direct effects of economic growth, were not strong enough to raise the suicide rate during the post-war period, as they did in the nineteenth century. There must therefore have been something else about growth in the *Trente Glorieuses* that had the effect of lowering the suicide rate. What was it and how can we identify it?

. . . And protective factors: creative individualism

Since the 1990s, a group of researchers led by Ronald Inglehart, Professor of Political Science at the University of Michigan, has been trying to list the moral values that inspire the inhabitants of a large number of countries (Inglehart and Baker 2000; Inglehart 2000). Their surveys cover large populations. And whilst the cavalier views of their authors sometimes look more like an intellectual free-for-all than a serious sociology of ethics, their questionnaires do include more than one pertinent question about sociability, trust in public services, views on the death penalty or authority in education, and they do allow more light to be shed on the sociological and ethical problem of suicide. They also use two axes to outline a suggestive cartography of the different dominant systems of values in different countries (Fig. 4.5, page 71).

The vertical axis is concerned mainly with the importance of religion in individuals' lives, with their desire to make their parents proud of them, the belief in heaven and hell, and attitudes towards

Figure 4.5 World distribution of values

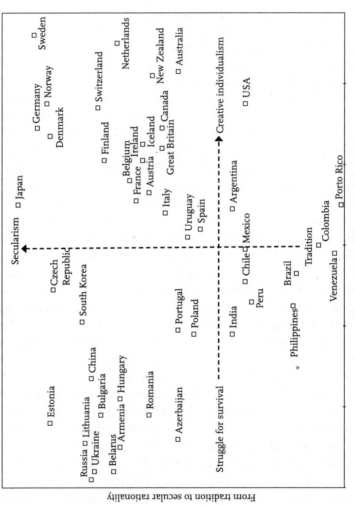

Source: R. Inglehart, *World Values Surveys*, 1995 and 1999.

euthanasia and suicide. In 'traditionalist' countries, the majority defines itself with reference to religion and strongly condemns euthanasia, suicide and divorce. It tends to be in favour of restrictions on immigration and is on the right of the political spectrum. 'Secular-rational' countries, in contrast, are characterized by the diametrically opposite positions they hold on all these problems: the majority of citizens are not shocked by euthanasia, divorce, suicide, etc.

The horizontal axis is primarily concerned with the meaning of work. On the left, we see the values of the 'struggle for survival' shared by countries in which the majority, unhappy with its material situation, regards work merely as a source of income and security, relegates the personal interest taken in work and its social aspects to a position of secondary importance, and takes the view that the primary goal of education is to teach children to work hard. Anything that places obstacles in the path of these materialist goals is violently rejected.

At the opposite extreme are the countries where priority is given to personal development both at school and at work, and where the emphasis is on a morality of tolerance and respect for others, and a firm belief in the superiority of democracy. Ronald Inglehart uses the generic term 'creative individualism' to describe all those values which, unlike the simple values of the 'struggle for survival', help to increase the importance of the individual and to construct the collective on the basis of the recognition of personal qualities and skills. This is a very different notion of individualism to that criticized by Durkheim. Far from being a factor that dissolves older earlier communities, the growing importance accorded to creative individualism no longer contrasts the individual with the group, but rather recognizes everyone's contribution to the dynamic construction of the group. These values of increased self-esteem are most obvious in the world of work. Work ceases to be regarded as just a way of making a living and becomes a form of self-realization and a source of personal satisfaction. A good job is a job that allows personal self-affirmation, and that allows the man or woman who does it to be creative and innovative, and even to 'have a ball'. When conditions are favourable, work becomes a source of happiness, even for the individual. The individual has the feeling that he or she is creating something that will last, that will be of service to others, and that will allow his or her true worth to be recognized. The individual will therefore be able to express the deepest and most creative paths of his or her personality by revealing them. The ordinary worker becomes an artist. The most important criterion now becomes the interest in work – an object in which the individual has a large personal investment. This new idea of a relationship with work, seen as an expression of oneself, is easily recognizable as an effect of the new forms of organization associated with the rise of the tertiary sector and the high grey-matter content of work in rich countries, especially for those who are in skilled managerial and supervisory positions (Baudelot, Gollac, Bessière, Coutant, Godechot, Serre and Viguier 2003). In more general terms, modern forms of work organization in the rich countries – which are increasingly dominated by the tertiary sector and becoming less and less industrialized – give individuals greater autonomy within the work process; they require greater personal investment and ask them to demonstrate the initiative they were prevented from taking in the past. The social system thus calls for personal creativity, and it is individualism that creates the social bond. This may well be a type of divorce, but it is also a way of restructuring the family.

The relationship between the suicide rate and each dimension of these value systems is informative. The vertical axis holds no surprises: the move away from religious, family and political traditions leads to a rise in the suicide rate. As Durkheim's analyses predicted, the most highly evolved societies, which give the individual priority over the group, have higher suicide rates. As the richest societies are usually the least traditional, we see here one of the perverse effects of development. These findings are perfectly consistent with those we have just described: divorce, falling fertility rates and the decline in religious observance encourage suicide (Fig. 4.6, page 74).

The very different correlation with the second axis is of much greater interest because it is new. The more closely work is associated with self-fulfilment and sociability in any given country, the more it ceases to be just a way of making a living and the suicide rate falls. The development of creative individualism partly compensates for the protection modern societies lose as they stray away from tradition. Once again, the correlation becomes more pronounced if we assume a constant level of wealth. Countries that have freed themselves from tradition but still see work solely in terms of a means of survival are penalized in two ways, as is the case for the countries of the former Socialist bloc.

If we locate it within Inglehart's cartography, the suicide rate looks like a very instructive spiral.

- The suicide rate is lowest in those poor countries that combine a high level of traditionalism and survival values: 0.6 per 100,000 in Peru, 2.5 in the Philippines and 5.4 in Mexico.

Figure 4.6 From traditional to secular values

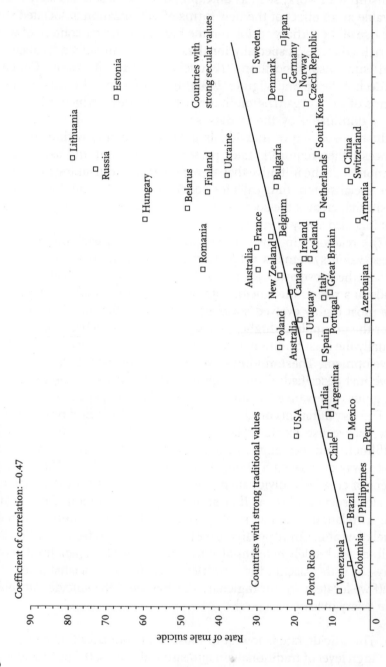

Coefficient of correlation: –0.47

Source: R. Inglehart, *World Values Surveys*, 1995 and 1999.

- In rich countries that remain strongly attached to tradition, we find suicide rates that are higher but relatively low, given their level of wealth. This is the case in Great Britain (11 per 100,000), Italy and the United States (almost 13).
- Rates are higher in those countries that combine a low degree of traditionalism with creative individualism, as creativity does not fully compensate for the loss of protection that results from the departure from tradition: this is true of France (30.4) and the countries of northern Europe (Sweden: 30.9; Finland 43.4; Denmark 24.2).
- Rates are highest, finally, in those countries that combine the absence of protection associated with an erosion of tradition with the persistence of survival values (Estonia: 67.3; Lithuania: 79.1 and Hungary: 59.9).

Relying on the data collected by Inglehart, one Canadian researcher set out to isolate the specific effect of disposable per capita income on suicide. Making an analysis of 117 countries, John F. Helliwell, a professor of economics at the University of Vancouver, attempted (2004) to evaluate the individual effect of five main variables on suicide that are usually correlated:

- sociability,
- trust in others,
- belief in God,
- level of divorce,
- per capita national income.

He was thus able to evaluate the effect of each of these variables on suicide when the others remain unchanged. His findings are as follows.

Other things being equal, sociability, trust in others and belief in God reduce the risk of suicide; rising divorce rates increase it, and per capita wealth has in itself a protective effect. We are therefore a long way from Durkheim's remarks about the protective effect of poverty. Wealth in fact seems to have a direct protective effect; it also has indirect protective effects, as sociability and trust in others are more marked in rich countries than in poor countries. Economic growth also has the effect of removing certain protective factors because, broadly speaking, it undermines religious belief and encourages divorce.

It is clear that these opinion polls about 'world values' suffer from certain weaknesses, and in particular a pronounced North American ethnocentrism. The same criterion for religious practice (*Go to church* . . .) is applied to all countries, irrespective of whether we are talking about protestant churches, Buddhist temples, Hindu places of worship or mosques. The values recorded and identified by the questionnaires have more to do with the extrapolation on a world scale of opinions that are widespread in Western countries than with the ethnological fieldwork that reveals the distinctive features of how different peoples view the world, and public and personal morality. The primacy given to comparability and to tables that place every country in the world within the same range of values leads to some very damaging simplifications. However, without taking the results too literally, this survey allows us to reinterpret the evolution of suicide amongst the rich nations, since the questionnaires lend themselves well to this. The confirmation that there is a strong link between suicide and forms of emancipation from traditional values (agnosticism, divorce and so on) explains why it is that, even during periods of growth, the suicide rate remains high in developed countries and never returns to the low levels around which it hovered prior to the industrial revolution of the nineteenth century. The rise of individualism, which is both a result of capitalist economic development and also one of its preconditions, does indeed introduce factors that lead to suicide.

This initial finding must not, however, be allowed to conceal another, which suggests a need for more in-depth studies. The rise of values associated with self-realization and creative individualism in rich countries, especially in the professional sphere, may attenuate or even cancel out the negative effects of primary individualism. The same inversion occurred in the case of urbanization during the first half of the twentieth century. The big towns and cities increased the risk of suicide in the nineteenth century, and reduced it in the twentieth. As they became more affluent, developed societies were able to discover new forms of social existence, both in the towns and at work, that were very different to those prevailing in villages communities centred around the church. These generated solidarity and did not necessarily lead to isolation. Largely overlooked by Durkheim in his analyses of suicide, the world of work now represents a strategic domain where, in contradictory fashion, a whole set of relations are forged between the individual and society, and in which the individual plays an important role. Professional activity makes up major element in both the social identity of individuals, as seen by others, and in their personal identities: the pressure to identify one's person with one's profession is so great that we say 'I *am* a teacher', 'I *am* a high-speed train driver' and 'I *am* a check-out assistant'. The growing pressure of new forms of organization encourages all workers to become more personally involved in their jobs and transforms success or failure into an existential verdict. When workers are required to become more personally involved in their projects, they come to believe that, should things go wrong, they alone are responsible. Those who do succeed, on the other hand, find that their professional success increases their self-confidence and self-belief, and fills them with new vigour.

This is why the suicide rate fell in certain developed countries and failed to rise in others during the periods of euphoric planned growth they experienced after the Second World War. To use basic Durkheimian vocabulary, the new forms of economic development and work were able to create new forms of integration between individuals. The investigations of Ronald Inglehart and all the developments he attributes to creative individualism and the appreciation of forms of self-expression teach us another important lesson. Although he does not have a word to say about it, the new forms of individualism he describes are not found, and are not shared, at every level of the social pyramid in the developed countries. Being happy at work implies that a whole series of preconditions for self-realization is present. These preconditions are more commonly found in well-paid, intellectual and graduate professions that guarantee job security than amongst casual workers or the staff of fast food outlets. Our professional contribution is more easily recognized when there is a balance between what we give and what we receive. Money does not make anyone happy, but it does a lot to make us feel happy at work. Indeed, those who say they are happiest at work are, leaving aside the clergy, the liberal professions, senior managers, company bosses and teachers. These are all professions that enjoy social prestige, and have a wide scope for initiative at work, and not least the freedom of having been able to choose their profession. They encourage self-expression and enjoy great prestige in the eyes of the public (Baudelot, Gollac *et al.* 2003). It is therefore the higher echelons of advanced societies that benefit from the most positive effects of economic development in the strategic domains of self-confidence, gratification of the ego and good social integration. It is not surprising that those categories at the top of the ladder are now the best protected from the risk of suicide, which was not the case in the twentieth century. We will consider this again later.

There is therefore no longer any direct link between economic development and the suicide rate in the twentieth century. There is a

Figure 4.7 From survival values to values of self-expression

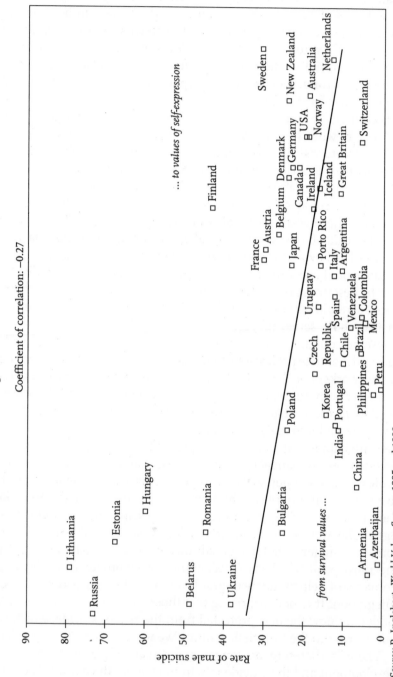

Coefficient of correlation: −0.27

Source: R. Inglehart, *World Values Surveys*, 1995 and 1999.

lot of data to suggest that, in the nineteenth century, it was not development itself that was directly responsible, but all the social upheavals that were associated with it, either as preconditions or effects. In those societies where the logic of development is more predictable, people can etch their personal strategies upon it: greater affluence no longer leads to an inevitable and continuous rise in the rates of suicide (Fig. 4.7, page 78[1]). The suicide rate remains high but no longer rises. At least so long as growth is sustained . . .

---

[1] The abscissas in Fig. 4.7 correspond to the positions of countries Inglehart identifies on the basis of the factorial analysis shown in Fig. 4.5. They refer to various countries' positions on the horizontal axis of the graph.

5   The Soviet Exception

The countries of the former Soviet bloc now have a very special place in the 'geography of despair', to use the expression of INED demographer Jean-Claude Chesnais (Chesnais 1981). They are in first place. According to the data collected by the World Health Organization (WHO), that position is stable and has not been altered by the publication of more recent statistics. With a male suicide rate of 79.1 per 100,000, Lithuania is ahead of all the other countries, and is immediately followed by Russia (72.9), Estonia (64.3), Kazakhstan, Hungary, Belarus, Slovenia, Finland, Ukraine and Moldova. The suicide rates recorded for the first three countries are more than twice as high as those observed in France (30.0) for the same period. The figures for the rest ensure that the countries of the former Soviet bloc have the unique distinction of leading the international pack. The women are not far behind the men. Whilst they are between two and five times less likely than men to take their own lives, the highest rates for suicide amongst women in the world are, with the exception of Sri Lanka, to be found in Lithuania, Hungary, Estonia, Slovenia, Russia and Finland.

The world leader

This position of international leader is, as we have seen, paradoxical, as it is a conspicuous exception to the close correlation observed at international level between a country's wealth at any given moment and its suicide rate. In the picture of an economic sky structured by suicide, dark clouds gather as nations' levels of wealth increase, and the countries of the former Soviet bloc generate a very impressive cumulonimbus at the bottom of the ladder of economic wealth. Despite having a fairly low GDP of between $3,000 and $5,000, they all have high suicide rates.

Table 5.1   Today, blue ribbon workers

Male suicide rates (per 100,000, 1995)		Female suicide rates (per 100,000, 1995)	
Lithuania	79.1	Sri Lanka	16.8
Russia	72.9	Hungary	16.7
Estonia	64.3	Lithuania	15.6
Kazakhstan	51.9	Estonia	14.1
Hungary	50.6	Slovenia	13.9
Belarus	48.7	Russia	13.7
Slovenia	45.3	Switzerland	12.2
Sri Lanka	44.6	Finland	11.8
Finland	43.4	Japan	11.3
Ukraine	38.2	Denmark	11.2
Moldova	30.9	Belgium	11
Switzerland	30.9	France	10.8
France	30.4	Singapore	10.5
Austria	30	Austria	10
Croatia	29.7	Croatia	9.8
		Bulgaria	9.7
		Belarus	9.6
		Kazakhstan	9.5
		Ukraine	9.2
		Hong Kong	9.2
		Sweden	9.2

It is clear that the GDP of these countries is a poor reflection of their real level of development. This is partly because of the way GDP used to be calculated in countries where market regulation was of secondary importance because a low level of productivity could be associated with very high levels of education and forward-looking health policies (services that are all difficult to evaluate in terms of GDP), partly because of the collapse of their national currencies and partly, finally, because of the sudden economic crises that forced output to fall without necessarily destroying society's standard of living. And there is a strong suspicion that it is the quality of development that is the causal link between GDP and suicide rates.

The underlying question remains. Why do the countries of the former socialist bloc have the distinction of having higher suicide rates than all the other countries in the world?

There is one obvious answer: alcohol. The reason why so many Russians kill themselves is that they drink too much vodka. Vodka adds a Slavic touch to the Russian suicide rate. Vodka fuels the most widespread explanations for the impressive rise in suicide in Russia in the second half of the twentieth century. It even takes a scientific and well argued form in various academic publications. Impressive and widely published graphs supposedly provide irrefutable proof of the existence of a causal link. The curves for the suicide rate and alcohol consumption are parallel. The more people drink, the more suicides there are. When alcohol is in short supply or becomes more expensive, the suicide rate falls accordingly (see Fig. 5.1, page 84).

The curve for the consumption of alcohol does indeed closely follow that for suicide and, more generally, that for violent death. Although both curves show an overall increase, they also record a spectacular fall between 1985 and 1987. The number of suicides and violent deaths and the rate of alcohol consumption all show the same downward trend. Why? The answer most often cited points to the measure taken by the Gorbachev government. The government cut the levels of state-controlled production and consumption of alcohol, raised prices, limited the number of private licences for distilling vodka and developed specialized medical services. These measures were enough to reduce the consumption of alcohol and, therefore, the number of violent deaths. Launched in 1985, this widespread anti-alcohol campaign lasted for less than two years. By the end of 1987, the Soviet government decided to increase the production of alcohol once more. The consumption of alcohol and the number of murders, suicides and other violent forms of death then resumed their steep rise, and provided irrefutable proof that there is a direct causal link between alcoholism and suicide. The more people drink, the more suicides there are. The less they drink, the fewer suicides there are.

This explanation is, however, somewhat inconclusive. To maintain, as INED's statisticians state in their study (Meslé *et al.* 1992 and 1996), that 'the rise in violent deaths in Russia is closely related to that of the consumption of alcohol' is an obvious fact. The statisticians are very careful not to take the further step of inferring the existence of a causal link because none of the available data allow them to do so. Correlation and causality are not the same thing.

A better way to approach the problem is to take into account the historical dimension of the phenomenon of suicide and try to identify the moment in time when all the countries of the former USSR began to lead the world in suicide. It is, however, difficult to supply a specific answer to that question, as there are no reliable long-term statistical series for these countries. In the case of Russia, there is in fact a black hole from the late 1920s until the second half of the 1960s. For

Figure 5.1 Comparative evolution of deaths from violence and consumption of alcohol, Russia, 1971–1993

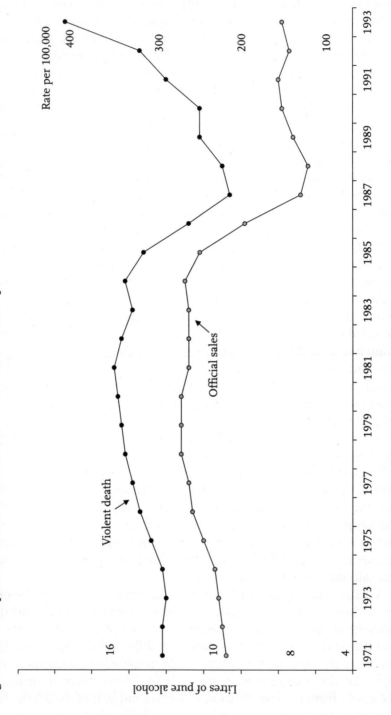

Source: F. Meslé et al., *La Crise sanitaire dans les pays de l'ex-URSS, 1965–1994*, INED, 1996.

forty-five years, there were no available statistics on suicide in Russia and, more generally, there were no data on the causes of death. The same is also true for most of the Socialist Republics once they entered the Soviet orbit, with the notable exception of Hungary, which kept up its own tradition. The number of suicides was a state secret, as was the number of deaths from cholera, epidemics, industrial accidents and homicide.

Anatomy of society and black-out

This was not always thus. The question of suicide in Russia was the subject of very lively scientific and public debates between those scientists and activists who were most committed to the revolutionary process (Ledina 1999; Pinnow 2000). The demographers, statisticians, forensic doctors and Party leaders involved in the debate were all greatly impressed by Durkheim's book and studied it in great detail. They were convinced that the explanation for suicide lay in its social causes, and that the phenomenon of suicide provided a good indicator of the state of the social, economic and political health of a nation. The wave of suicides that followed the failed revolution of 1905 was widely discussed. Responsibility was very quickly laid at the door of the State on the grounds that state repression had stood in the way of people's prospects. Demographers were alarmed to find that, far from falling, suicide rates had tended to rise considerably after 1917 in the big cities, especially in Leningrad. At the end of the nineteenth century, the suicide rate was low (about 13 per 100,000 in St Petersburg between 1881 and 1900). It rose sharply after 1905 (38.5 in 1910) and then fell considerably during the war, with a low of 10.5 per 100,000 in 1917. After that, there was a constant and spectacular rise in the capital: 15.4 in 1918, 31.8 in 1925, and 37.5 in 1928. At this point, Leningrad had the seventh highest suicide rate in the world. All these scientists, most of whom supported the Revolution, were convinced that a close study of the development of the phenomenon in Russia was essential, and that they needed to produce the most detailed and exhaustive social statistics possible. An in-depth study would make it possible to detect the social origins of the phenomenon and identify the political measure that would remedy the situation. Russian statisticians therefore began to evaluate the effects of the Revolution on the motives for suicide (the category 'changes in the material situation' figures alongside more classic reasons such as 'illness, nervous and mental disorders', 'loss of interest in life', 'love and jealousy'), as well as the effects on society ('*déclassé* groups' and 'independent professions' were listed alongside 'manual workers' and 'office workers').

At the end of the civil war, the People's Commissariat of Health for the Russian Republic commissioned a detailed questionnaire about suicides and attempted suicides. This statistical exercise began to cover the whole of the USSR from 1925 onwards, but only two volumes were published in Moscow in 1927 and 1929 under the auspices of the Division of Moral Statistics. The first volume covers successful suicides in the USSR between 1922 and 1925, and the second suicides recorded in 1925 and 1926. No trace of subsequent surveys has ever been found, but there is every indication that the plan was abandoned after 1926 (Rittersporn 1997). The data that were collected are, however, of great interest and provided much of the information for the chapter in Halbwachs's 1930 study devoted to the influence of the family situation on suicide.[1] Greatly influenced by Durkheim's book, the tables published analyse society in terms of the main variables identified by the French sociologist: place of residence, sex, age, marital status, month of the year and day of the week, motive, 'social class' and level of education. The social image of suicide that emerges from all these tables conforms very closely to the system of suicide, as analysed by Durkheim in most European countries at the end of the nineteenth century. There were more suicides in Leningrad and Moscow than in other cities, and many more in the towns than in the countryside. Twice as many men as women committed suicide; 'proprietors and members of the family helping in the business', 'officer workers' and in particular the 'independent professions' killed themselves much more often than the workers. Similarly, the suicide rate for people who had had an education (primary, secondary and higher) was much higher than that for the illiterate. The number of suicides was at its highest between April and August, and at its lowest in the autumn and winter months. There were more suicides on Mondays than on other days, and most occurred between ten in the morning and three in the afternoon. Suicide was less frequent amongst married people than amongst the single, and in families with children than amongst childless couples. Maurice Halbwachs relied heavily upon these data, which he studied in detail in order to demonstrate that children had a protective role; Durkheim had abandoned the attempt for

---

[1] Halbwachs (1930), Chapter 8: 'Suicide and the family, the effect of the number of children: the Russian experience' (151–155).

Table 5.2   Suicide rates in USSR per 100,000, 1925

	Men	Women
Leningrad	43.1	20.2
Moscow	31.2	14.5
Other towns	27.6	13.6
Countryside	5.7	2.6
Total	11.3	6.0

Source: *Suicides en URSS, 1922–1925*, Section de la statistique morale, vol. XXXV, Livraison 1, Moscow, 1927, p. 14.

lack of adequate data. Their state of marriage as such did less to protect women than men from suicide, but married women and men both enjoyed a greater degree of protection if they had children, and the degree of protection increased as the number of children rose, especially in the case of women. Urban suicides, suicides amongst educated people and those in 'independent' occupations (who were neither workers nor salaried staff) meant that suicide affected the intellectual sections of society more than others. The Soviet picture displays the same profile as the countries of Western Europe in the late nineteenth century.

There were, however, three differences. Despite the alarmist debate of political leaders and officials, the suicide rate in the Soviet Union was quite low in 1922–25; the rate of 11.3 for men and 6.0 for women was closer to that of England rather than the high rate prevailing in France at the same time. Its low levels and the very minor variations observed between the days of the week reflected what was still a very rural stage of economic development. The gap between the towns and the countryside was huge, and the peasant populations, which were by far the largest, greatly reduced the average suicide rate, which was below 10 per 100,000. What is more striking is that suicide in the Soviet Union was more widespread amongst young people, especially in the big cities, than amongst old people (12.4 per 100,000 for 18- to 19-year-olds, 14.4 for 20- to 24-year-olds, as against 7.7 for 30- to 39-year-olds, and 5.8 for those over 60). Suicides also usually occurred at night, which goes against the data collected in France and other European countries.

Politicized statisticians were not the only ones to be concerned about the suicide question at this time. It also gave rise to many debates amongst forensic medical examiners (Pinnow 2000). Two currents of opinion emerged: one social, and the other somatic. According to Iakov Leonovich Leibovich, the uncontested leader of the 'social' tendency, 'Forensic medicine should not limit itself to the autopsy of dead bodies and the investigation of living ones, but to a proper measure it should put its efforts into the business of studying and constructing social life' (cited in Pinnow 2000: 122). Its goal was to identify those subjects in the practice of forensic medicine that had real implications for the well-being and development of the population as a whole. Hence the interest in moral statistics, which were primarily devoted to phenomena that were thought to best reflect the moral tenor of a culture: abortion, crime, murder and suicide. These forensic doctors thought that they were especially well placed to undertake an exhaustive analysis of the Soviet social order, to diagnose the underlying causes of social pathology and to work to eradicate them. Leibovich (cited in Pinnow 2000: 128) writes:

> In the same way that the palæontologist can reproduce in his imagination an entire antediluvian animal on the basis of a single part of a skeleton, for example, a femur [. . .] so, too, the sociologist, on the basis of a single group of phenomena or one link in the chain of social facts, is often capable of providing the characterization of the given society. That is what interests us about suicide.

As he pursued his argument, Leibovich was the first to discover that Soviet society differed from both Western societies and *ancien régime* Russia in one significant respect: the gap between female and male suicides was smaller. One woman committed suicide for every two men in Russia, whereas the female/male ratio was equal to or greater than one to three in the countries of Western Europe. In his view, the rising number of women who committed suicide was a clear and empirical sign that Russian women had been emancipated during the revolutionary period (cited in Pinnow 2000: 131):

> Woman does not enjoy equality of rights in any other country. Nowhere else does she participate so intensely in social life. Only a social revolution having carried out a re-evaluation of all values and having made human labour the cornerstone of all interrelations could provide such equal rights.

'A woman pays a high price for the equalization in civil rights' (cited in Pinnow 2000: 131) because, having lost the protection afforded to housewives by their families and children, they were more exposed to the risk of suicide. One might think this is a strange way of assessing the benefits of the revolution, but the fact remains that these forensic doctors saw suicide as a relevant symptom of the profound transformations in society. The emphasis was not so much on the phenomenon itself as on the social factors that gave rise to it.

At the same time, a different current within Soviet forensic medicine adopted the opposite point of view. Those doctors who supported a biological explanation for human behaviour were convinced that there was nothing social about suicide. Differences in the form and structure of an individual's organism were the only things that could explain why certain people chose to kill themselves, whilst others who were subject to the same external constraints did not do so. The source of the mystery lay somewhere in the brains of the individuals concerned. These forensic doctors did not claim that external factors did not contribute to the formation of a suicidal personality. They simply refused to ascribe a primary or principal role to these factors. It was only because internal morphological changes had weakened the individual psyche and its defence mechanisms that marital disharmony, the loss of a job and other social factors had such devastating effects.

Alexandre Ivanovich Kriukov, Director of the Moscow Department of Forensic Medicine and one of the strongest supporters of the somatic paradigm, clearly sums up the interaction between biological and social factors (cited in Pinnow 2000: 119): 'The root cause of suicides lies in the physical organization of the subject, who for the time being copes with the condition of life . . . external causalities can play, although not always, only the role of a spark or stimulus.' Autopsy therefore becomes the essential tool: 'That which was previously dark and incomprehensible now, under the study of the tissues and organs of the corpses of suicides, becomes fully explicable' (cited: 121).

Kriukov and his disciples in fact claimed to have detected in the bodies of suicides signs and stigmata that revealed that the brain had degenerated as a result of a mismatch between the size of the brain and that of the skull cavity. Either the brain was floating in the skull cavity, or it was too compressed. The answer was to be found in the phenomena of adhesions: in a severe tension in the dura mater, or in the excessive volume of the cerebral mass compared with individuals of the same sex and age: 'With knife in hand at the dissection table, the pathological anatomist and the legal doctor have attempted to solve the mystery of death' (cited: 120).

These were not isolated illusions. Many Bolsheviks thought that scientific progress might one day make men immortal, and the embalming of the bodies of their leaders, especially Lenin, were part of that wait-and-see strategy (Tartarin 2004).

All these debates and projects led nowhere. The social significance ascribed to suicide by the political authorities was suddenly reversed. Taking the opposite attitude to the Orthodox Church, which condemned suicide and refused to accept the bodies of suicides in its churches and cemeteries, the Bolsheviks had initially shown greater tolerance to suicides, their families and those who had tried to kill themselves. That attitude, which was largely inspired by their anticlerical views, reflected a desire to promote a more democratic notion of individual freedom. They regarded suicide as a social phenomenon which, whilst it was certainly deviant (Ledina 1999; Rittersporn 1997), occurred mainly because life had lost its meaning; the individuals concerned were not necessarily responsible.

The suicide rate then went up under the NEP.[2] Even Party members were affected. Suicide was responsible for 13% of deaths amongst Party members in the first four months of 1925. Suicides by Party members accounted for about 7% of all suicides recorded throughout the country in 1925; their suicide rate was, in other words, some ten times higher than might be expected, given the percentage of Party members in the population as a whole. Trotsky's former secretary committed suicide. Suicide within the ranks of the Party was, however, only one part of the question. Although the Soviet suicide rate was still much lower than that of Western countries at the end of the 1920s (it was below 10 per 100,000 in the USSR, whereas it hovered between 20 and 30 in France), the rate amongst young people was worrying because, in contrast with the trends recorded in other countries, rates were very high amongst 20- to 24-year-olds, followed by 16- to 19-year-olds and 25- to 29-year-olds. This was true for both men and women, and for both the towns and the countryside (Ledina 1999; Rittersporn 1997).

The tone of the official debate on suicide changed. Faced with that they called a 'new epidemic', Party leaders and People's Commissars at first insisted on seeing the phenomenon as a relic from a past condemned to disappear in the near future. It was attributed to 'dying' social classes and to the influence of their decadent ideology. This 'explanation', which was still couched in social terms, was enough to dissuade the authorities from undertaking a statistical study of the phenomenon. But the debate very quickly became radicalized. It became individualized. The emphasis was now on psychological and individual causes and suicide was stigmatized and politically condemned as a result. At the 1925 Congress of the Bolshevik Party, suicides were described as people with fragile nerves and weak characters. A year later, following a special study of suicide amongst young people in Leningrad, the 'average suicide' became a 'whinging

---

[2] New Economic Policy: a series of reforms launched by Lenin in 1921.

intellectual with a penchant for self-flagellation'. When the wave of suicides began to affect workers, it was quickly asserted that those who committed suicide had no roots in 'revolutionary working-class youth'. The only people to commit suicide were the new *déclassés* faced with the reality of the working-class condition. The wave of suicides that followed that of Essenine, a poet especially popular with young people, was quickly condemned from a socio-political point of view. The spread of suicide was nothing more than the spread of a petty-bourgeois state of mind amongst individuals who simply abdicate all their responsibilities: 'Esseninery'. In 1928, the suicide of a young woman working at the Red Triangle factory in Leningrad was the object of a harsh verdict. The Komsomols (Young Communists) likened suicides to hooligans. 'Runt', 'abortion' and 'loner' were the labels often reserved for worker comrades who took their own lives.

Most Soviet newspapers reported suicides in the 'news in brief' section, alongside reports of theft, assault, drinking binges and brawls, and commented on them in the same critical way. The surnames of suicides were openly printed. In the issue of *Pravda* dated 1 September 1929, we can read an article listing those members of the Central Committee who had committed suicide and who had been accused of belonging to the Trotskyite opposition. The title is unequivocal: 'Leningrad's Communards must develop bolder forms of self-criticism and stamp out concrete manifestations of right-wing opportunism.' In the collective consciousness, suicide was coming to look more and more like a shameful form of behaviour. When Stalin's son Yakov attempted suicide in the spring of 1928, Stalin reacted in a letter to his wife: his son had behaved like a hooligan and a black-mailer, and he wanted nothing more to do with him. He reacted in the same way when his wife killed herself in 1931. It was made to look as though she had died from illness.

In 1936, at a time when many officials threatened by the purges thought voluntary death preferable to arrest, 'the supreme authority is at pains to assert before officials from leading bodies, in one of the plenary sessions of the Central Committee, that suicide is a form of treason against the Party, and probably proves that the probity of anyone who resorts to it was not above all suspicion' (Rittersporn 1997).

Suicide and industrialization: a forced march

This change in the political attitude towards suicide – what was once social had now become individual again – helped to bury the relevant

Table 5.3   Suicide rates in USSR per 100,000 and GDP, 1925 and 1965

	Male suicide rate	Female suicide rate	Per capita GDP (constant $90)
1925	11.3	6.0	1,370
1965	37.0	9.0	4,634

public statistics. We know that, once the civil war was over, the police began to keep their own statistics and that the scores recorded were, even before 1924, much higher than those in the questionnaires overseen by the National Statistics Directorate. A directive from the police High Command in April 1933 required all station commanders to send the forms that had to be completed for each suicide to Moscow twice a year. The very detailed questionnaires included 'social position' and, where applicable, Party membership. It seems, however, that the 1933 directive remained a dead letter: it was feared that it would give a negative image of how society was developing. Even assuming that the forms were completed and sent off, they were never analysed. The figures for criminality, the concentration camps and political offences are also very patchy. For the moment, we therefore have no reliable data on the evolution of suicide in Russia from the mid-1920s (1922–26) to the early 1960s. Even so, and despite these gaps in the statistical data, it is apparent that suicide rates rose very steeply. The rise coincided with rapid industrialization.

The male suicide rate rose from 11.3 to 37.0 per 100,000, i.e. it evolved from 100 to 330, whilst the female rate rose from 6.0 to 9.0, evolving from 100 to 151. At the time when Durkheim was observing and deploring the high suicide rate throughout Europe, he never observed such large-scale variations over a period of forty years. In fact between 1871 and 1911, the suicide rate rose from 100 to 178 in France, from 100 to 154 in Great Britain, and from 100 to 240 in Italy. In the nineteenth century, suicide rates in Britain and France certainly went hand in hand with considerable sacrifices – women and children working, the exodus from the countryside, etc. – but neither country ever recorded suicide rates as high as those associated with the forced industrialization of the USSR. The low Russian suicide rate for 1925 concerned a country with a very low level of economic development: between 1900 and 1913 per capita GDP rose at a rate of 1%. And in 1925, the rate of growth was lower than in 1913. Between 1928 and 1965, per capita wealth grew at a rate of 3.3%. As a result of this development, the level of wealth achieved by the

USSR was roughly equivalent to that of Great Britain in 1922 and that of France in 1926. The sudden impact of a modern industrial society had the same effects on Russia as the development of capitalism in nineteenth-century Europe: the suicide rate rose. But the way in which change had occurred meant that its effects were more widespread.

And then there was light . . . long live French demography!

It is only recently that this politically instigated mist has begun to clear – in the case of Russia at least. A great deal of work has been done by a team of demographers from INED, working in collaboration with researchers at Moscow's Centre for Demography and Human Ecology (Meslé, Shkolnikov, Hertrich and Vallin 1992, 1996). They have succeeded in reconstructing a homogeneous series of detailed statistics on the causes of death in Russia between 1965 and 1995 by applying the INED statisticians' and demographers' vast experience of analysing causes of death and life expectancy to a mine of information consisting of almost two thousand original manuscript tables drawn up by Russian civil servants. They are at present doing the same for each of the fifteen Republics that once made up the Soviet Union. Their goal is to make an in-depth analysis of the 'health crisis' that affected the USSR in the last decades of its existence. Between 1965 and 1994, life expectancy at birth actually fell by five years in Russia, whereas it rose sharply in all Western countries.

The principal interest of these completely new statistics is to set the rising suicide rate against the general context of a decline in life expectancy. Until the Second World War, life expectancy at birth remained far below the levels achieved by Western countries. It was 32 years in 1896–97, whereas in both France and the United States it had increased to 47 years. The fifteen-year discrepancy remained stable and even increased during the first half of the twentieth century: on the eve of the first World War, life expectancy in Russia had reached 43 years, as against 59 years in France and 63 years in the United States. There was, however, a considerable improvement just after the war that brought Russia into line with France and the United States: 64.3 years for men in 1965, as against 67.5 in France and 66.8 in the United States; life expectancy was 73.4 years for women, as against 74.7 and 73.7, respectively.

From 1970 onwards, the curves for life expectancy began to diverge. Whereas there was a sustained rise in France and the United States, life expectancy remained constant or declined in Russia, particularly for men.

In order to elucidate and better understand the causes of this 'health crisis', the authors make a very detailed analysis of changes in the mortality rate in Russia between 1965 and 1995, breaking the figures down by sex, age and cause of death. The great leap forward in life expectancy achieved in Russia between 1945 and 1964 is mainly attributable to the fall in the mortality rate for young people under 15 years of age. After 1965, the spectacular increase in life expectancy observed in France, the United States and Japan stems from the fall in the mortality rate for those over 60. It stems, in other words, from the advances made by Western medicine in its fight against cardiovascular diseases, cancers and problems relating to the accelerating rate of economic change: alcoholism, smoking-related illnesses and road accidents. The Russians failed to find this 'second wind'. Although child and juvenile mortality rates were reduced during the two post-war decades, the second stage of the rocket did not fall away. The risk of dying after the age of 15 rose sharply, especially for men aged between 30 and 59. The worsening position of males aged 15 and over reduced male life expectancy by over six years between 1965 and 1993. The male suicide rate for men is, according to the authors, now the highest in the world. Already visible in about 1958, it has risen constantly and sharply since then, and it accelerated from 1989 onwards.

Three main causes of death explain more than 80% of deaths during this period: cardiovascular disease (over 50% of deaths amongst men, and 65% amongst women), cancer (16 to 18% of all deaths) and violent deaths – alcohol poisoning, falls, drowning, road accidents, murder and suicide. Deaths from violent causes caught up with and then overtook cancer for the first time in 1993. The proportion of adults who died from these three causes rose constantly between 1965 and 1995, whereas there was a significant fall in deaths from infectious and gastrointestinal diseases.

Suicide rates rose sharply during this period, rising from 37 to 76 per 100,000 for men and from 9 to 13.7 for women. The male rate at the beginning of this period is high, but remains close to the levels in European countries with high suicide rates. France, Germany and Denmark experienced similar levels at the end of the nineteenth century and the beginning of the twentieth. The same is not true of the levels reached at the end of the same period; they, together with those for Lithuania, are unprecedented world records (Ruzicka 1996).

Several lessons emerge from the new and valuable statistics drawn up by INED and Moscow's Centre for Demography and Human Ecology.

Between 1965 and 1995, Russia's suicide rate rose steeply. It was quite low in the nineteenth century and remained so until almost the end of the 1920s, even though there was a marked contrast between the cities and the countryside. Leningrad was one of the great capitals where the number of suicides reached record levels. Almost nothing is known about how suicide rates in the USSR changed between the late 1920s and the early 1960s.

The steep increase in suicides during this period goes hand in hand with a decrease in life expectancy and an equally spectacular increase in deaths from cardiovascular diseases, but above all in violent deaths: accidents (especially road accidents), poisonings, accidents at work and homicides. Contrary to the somewhat primitive psychological theory elaborated by Morselli and then blithely adopted by other researchers, which holds that suicide and homicide vary in inverse proportion to each other, with violence towards others tending to replace violence directed at the self (and conversely), the two forms of violence increased at the same time, both here and in many other countries. The evolution of homicide was marked by two very big increases: between 1965 and 1981, deaths by homicide doubled for both men and women. In the six years from 1987 onwards, the homicide rate rose by almost 5 for men and 3 for women. For purposes of comparison, the Russian rate of death by homicide for men is thirty-four times higher than the rate observed in France. It is probably still underestimated: the concomitant explosion of 'violent deaths from undetermined causes', which rose at a very similar rate to deaths by homicide, suggest that a not inconsiderable number of the deaths attributed to this cause were in fact homicides and suicides. The wave of homicides is obviously bound up with an increase in delinquency, but it is also associated with an unprecedented increase in violent deaths in general – including suicide – that relate to the repercussions of economic 'reforms', declining standards of living and the disintegration of the old social and political order. Adult males and old people in general were badly affected. The greater vulnerability of this age group is quite obvious from Fig. 5.2 (page 96).

The suicide rate for all ages is rising, and has been rising very steeply since the end of the 1980s. Its rate of increase is greatest among men aged over 60 (from 100 to 212) and lowest for men aged between 20 and 29 (100 to 151). Those who suffer most from the

Figure 5.2   Evolution of male suicide rates by age, Russia, from 1965 to 1995

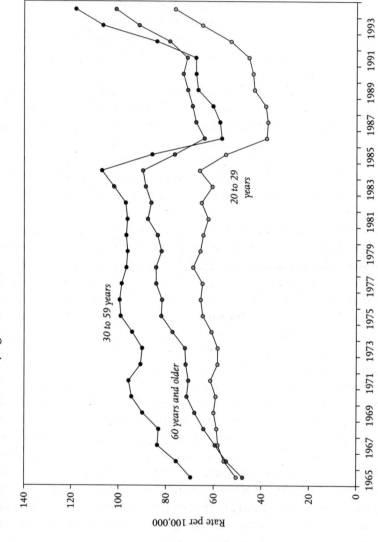

Source: F. Meslé *et al.*, *La Crise sanitaire dans les pays de l'ex-URSS, 1965–1994*, INED, 1996.

sudden changes in society are those who had a comfortable position under the Soviet regime (house, job and access to healthcare) and who suddenly find themselves deprived of all the protection it provided and who have no way of adapting to the new demands of a liberal economy which is now governed by the 'truth of prices', namely adults and old people.

Rather than regarding alcohol consumption as the ultimate cause of the rising suicide rate, we should, on the contrary, see it as an effect rather than a cause. Fig. 5.3 (page 98) is worthy of some consideration. The profiles for the evolution of a large number of violent deaths rise at the same rate: general accidents, alcoholism (deaths from cirrhosis and alcohol poisoning), suicides and homicides. They reveal an increasing level of violence, itself a symptom of how profoundly dysfunctional the workings of society have become. Drinking certainly increases the propensity to commit acts of violence, but it is also essential to ask why people begin to drink. Alcohol, like suicide, is a well-known way of escaping the miseries of everyday life. Such high suicide rates occur within the context of a general breakdown of society. Nothing works any more.

As for the fall in all indicators of violence in the period 1985–87, it should be seen as a moment of hope for society as a whole rather than simply as the result of measures restricting the volume of alcohol consumed and raising the price.

A careful examination of the evolution of suicide rates also reveals a marked discrepancy between two calendars. One is the social and political calendar that marks major events in a society with the seal of its important dates. Using this standard, the collapse of Soviet society dates from the fall of the Berlin wall (1989) and from the moment when Gorbachev created the Community of Independent States (1990). But the mortality statistics (Fig. 5.4, page 99) clearly indicate that the USSR began to experience a 'health crisis' from about 1965 onwards, a crisis that was the result of a whole series of large-scale breakdowns in the workings of Soviet society, which had continued all through its existence.

From the end of the Khrushchev era onwards, Soviet society began to be deeply undermined by contradictions and dysfunctions that its leaders could no longer control. Judging by the statistics for mortality and causes of death, it is clear that Soviet society began to disintegrate in the mid-1960s, or in other words almost thirty years before its political collapse. These health symptoms are not isolated: the rough divorce rate (the ratio between the number of divorces in any given

Figure 5.3 Deaths from violence, USSR and Russia, 1965–1995

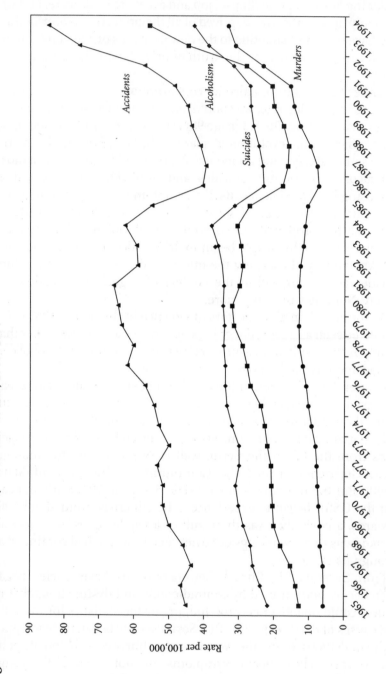

Source: F. Meslé et al., *La Crise sanitaire dans les pays de l'ex-URSS, 1965–1994,* INED, 1996.

Figure 5.4   Evolution of suicide rates in Russia (1965–1995)

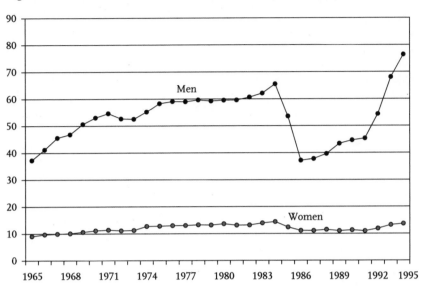

Source: F. Meslé *et al., La Crise sanitaire dans les pays de l'ex-URSS, 1965–1994,* INED, 1996.

year and the average population in the same year) rose from 1.4 in 1959 to 4.6 in 1994. The circumstantial indicator for divorce (the number of divorces divided by the number of marriages in the age classes concerned) recorded an even more spectacular rise. It rose from 25% at the beginning of the 1990s to 50% in 1993: one in two marriages ended in divorce (Avdeev and Monnier 1996).

One hundred years ago, its suicide rate placed Russia at the bottom of the international table. By the end of the twentieth century, it was at the top of the league. Compared with this enormous upheaval and judging by this very sensitive indicator, the industrial revolution that shook the countries of Western Europe so badly was no more than a minor earthquake. Weak beer, not vodka . . .

6   The Oil Crisis and Suicide amongst the Young

The most spectacular of all the transformations to have affected the pattern of suicide during the last two hundred years is concerned with age. The last quarter of the twentieth century completely overturned a connection which had come to be regarded as a universal fact as a result of over one hundred and fifty years of statistics gathered globally: suicide rates rise regularly as people grow older. There were no exceptions to this trend in the vast majority of countries for which statistics were available. Few young people took their own lives but the respective number of individuals who did so rose in almost linear fashion as they grew older. Because it had the force of a universally recognized and self-evident truth, the link attracted little comment. It was so simple and so universal that it had become transparent. Even though the discrepancies he observed between the youngest and oldest suicides was far greater than those he found when he considered marital status, religion or urbanization, Emile Durkheim never regarded age as a social fact in its own right. He simply saw the fact that the suicide rate rose as people grew older as further proof of the social nature of the phenomenon: the longer one spent living in society, the greater the risk of suicide. The causes of suicide were to be found in the life of society and its long-term effects on the individual, and not in nature or biology: 'How can we attribute this tendency to heredity, when it only appears in adults and, when it does appear, gathers in strength as the individual advances in age?' (Durkheim 1897: 90).

The length of time individuals are exposed to the effects of society is the only dimension Durkheim recognizes and he notes (1897: 360–361) that its effects vary greatly:

> We know in fact that this tendency [to commit suicide] grows from youth to maturity, and that it is often ten times stronger towards the end of life than at its start. This is because the collective forces that drive a man to kill himself only penetrate him little by little. Other things being equal,

it is as he gets older than he becomes more vulnerable, no doubt because repeated experiments are needed to make him feel the full emptiness of an egotistical existence or the utter vanity of boundless ambition.

So much for the content of the argument. As for its form, the use Durkheim makes of age in his analysis is purely as a statistical technique. In the course of his argument, age is used as a control variable that allows the effects of the other variables to be observed in a pure state: if, for example, more single people, the widowed and the divorced commit suicide than married people in all age groups, it is because marriage in itself has a protective effect. And age itself has nothing to do with it.

Demographers, sociologists and economists now pay more attention to the effects of age and generation on all aspects of society, and see now the way suicide rates vary with age as particularly significant. They have put forward various explanations for the almost linear increase in the risk of suicide as the years go by. The most common explanation confirms, in its own way, the principle behind Durkheim's explanation: ageing is likened to a 'social death',[1] since as they age people gather more factors that favour suicide: weakening of the bonds that relate individuals to the main sources of integration, such as the family (children leaving home, loneliness, losing a husband or wife . . .) and professional activity (retirement, the feeling of being useless, the loss of the regulated use of time and space used in commuting between home and work) and, until the recent past, impoverishment and material insecurity. According to certain economists (Hamermesh and Soss 1974), suicide can become a rational calculation of the balance between the costs and sufferings that are to be expected of a gloomier future and the slender benefits one can expect from the time one has left to live. The value expected from the future is lower than that of the deliverance from suffering brought about by death. Particularly as, given that at an advanced age life expectancy rapidly decreases, the length of life that would be sacrificed is much lower than that which an adolescent or a 20-year-old would have to make. The fact that the risk of suicide increases with age was put down to the various material conditions associated with the major stages of life in the nineteenth century and the first half of the twentieth. Old age was often an economic and physical shipwreck, whereas young people were able to

---

[1] This is the title (*La Retraite, une mort sociale*) of Anne-Marie Guillemard's study (1972) of retired people in the late 1960s.

Figure 6.1   Evolution of suicide rates by age, USA, from 1950–1990

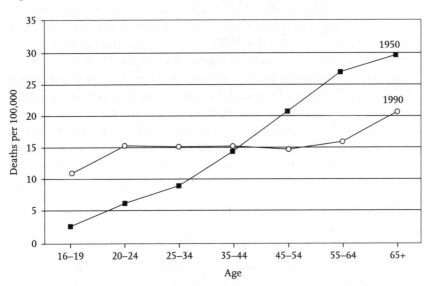

Source: D.M. Cutler, E.L. Glaeser and K.E. Norberg, 'Explaining the rise in youth suicide',
NBER, *Working Paper* no. 7713, 2004.

look forward to a prosperous future. Common sense theories thus
confirmed one of the most robust facts established by the sociology of
suicide, which became boring because it displayed no spatial or temporal variations.

However, this fine old institution that had been around for one
hundred and fifty years suddenly fell apart in the 1970s as a result of
two trends: there were more suicides amongst young people, and
fewer amongst the old. The two phenomena appeared at the same
point in time; they are closely related and must be analysed together.
There is now a gulf between the young and the old, and it is a gulf
between those who enjoy the main advantages of social power and
those who suffer the greatest number of handicaps.

The reversal of the trend takes a spectacular form in the United
States, where suicide rates have evened out. The suicide rate for young
people aged between 15 and 24 tripled in the second half of the twentieth century, whereas the rate for adults and old people fell during the
same period. Whereas it showed a strong rise in 1950, the age profile
of suicides aged between 20 and 65 had flattened out by 1990. For forty
years, the curve seems to have pivoted around the axis representing
the number of suicides amongst people aged between 35 and 44,
which remained constant (see Fig. 6.1 above).

The trend was the same in France. The suicide rate amongst young people rose as that for the elderly fell: in 1950, almost five times as many people aged between 65 and 74 committed suicide than those between 25 and 34, but by 1995 the ratio had fallen to 1.5. The symmetry is, however, less pronounced than in the United States: the curve does not change from a straight upward line to a horizontal one. It takes the form of a bimodal shape. These differences are highly instructive. Whilst the trend that emerged in the 1970s can be observed in all the developed countries, it takes specific forms in different countries that prove to be particularly informative. Jean-Claude Chesnais (1973) was the first to forecast the international trend towards a flattening out of suicide rates by age (see Fig. 6.2, page 105).

France: young people at risk, while the old are protected

We can begin by studying the forms taken by this trend in France, where a number of researchers have carried out a remarkable analysis of the phenomenon based on reliable data (Surault 1995a; Chauvel 1997; Anguis, Cases and Surault 2002). Let us remember that suicide rates, which remained relatively stable from the end of the Second World War until the first half of the 1970s, suddenly rose between 1976 and 1987, when they almost reached the historic peak recorded at the end of the nineteenth century and the end of the 1900s. Between 1976 and 1985, the male suicide rate rose by almost 45% from 22.9 per 100,000 to 33.1. The curve began to fall between 1985 and 1990 and then began to rise again until 1995. It then fell again, but remained much higher than the rate prevailing before the oil crisis. The rise was largely due to a large rise in suicides amongst men under 40. Other indicators displayed a similar trend during this period: youth unemployment, economic growth, people's opinions about French standards of living, delinquency and the age at which young people first got married. There is a close correlation (more than 0.80) between each of these developments and that of the suicide rate, in particular that between the rate of unemployment for young men aged between 15 and 24 and suicides in the male population as a whole. There are three possible explanations for this change. It could be influenced by age, by the period or by generation. Each of these hypotheses has been subjected to sophisticated tests. The most convincing findings, in particular those reached by Louis Chauvel, reject the generational explanation (some generations are more prone to suicide than others . . .)

Figure 6.2 Suicide rates by age, France, 1975–1985–1995

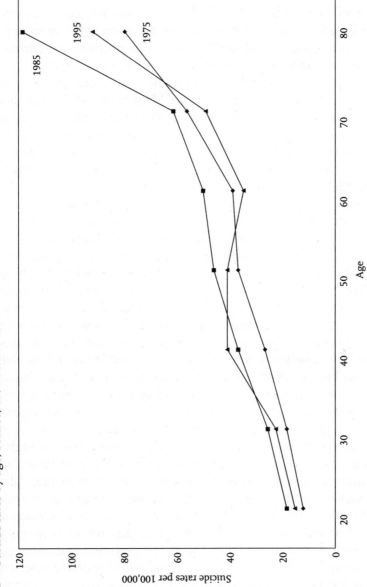

Source: L. Chauvel, *Revue française de sociologie*, no. XXXVIII, 4, 1997.

and explain most of these changes in terms of a combination of a life stage and a particular economic and social situation: 'The reasons why individuals despair of life are not the same and depend upon the age at which those individuals encounter this or that period in the history of their societies' (Chauvel 1997). Indeed, being 20 years old in 1975 and looking for a job when mass unemployment was becoming a permanent phenomenon did not have the same meaning as retiring in that year and knowing that you would receive almost 80% of your final salary for the rest of your days. Uncertainty and insecurity on the one hand, security on the other. As Karl Mannheim (1928) saw quite clearly, it is not so much the event in itself that matters as the age when we encounter it. We can therefore explain the change in the age profile of suicide in terms of the changes in the social content for people at different life stages caused by the new economic situation that emerged after the oil crisis in the 1970s.

As many studies have shown, a downturn in growth changes the social status of youth profoundly. For the vast majority of young people, an early introduction to the world of work that coincides with starting a family and setting up home independently has given way to a much later start to these life stages. The age at which young people complete their studies, find their first jobs, leave home, embark upon relationships and have their first child has gradually risen. This is true of all social categories. Youth is a life stage that is becoming longer without providing a human resource that is negotiable on the labour market. Over a period of thirty years, levels of qualification have risen, but it has become more difficult for those with qualifications to find work. During the thirty years of strong growth, in contrast, young people were employed on a 'rising salary' basis, with new entrants receiving higher starting salaries than their elders. This ensured that their salaries would, unlike those of their parents, rise throughout their careers. This mechanism broke down in the mid-1970s, with new entrants on salaries equal to, or lower than, those of their elders. At the same time, the wage differentials between age groups increased considerably, to the disadvantage of the young. These differences are a very clear reflection of a whole range of differences between the young and the rest in the field of work, employment and, more generally, life styles. Above all it is young people who inevitably experience the new forms of unemployment (and unemployment . . .) imposed by the new economic climate: lack of job security, casual work, job flexibility and the intensification of work, against a background of growing social and professional insecurity. One of the distinguishing features of young people is that their rate of unemployment is always much higher than that of other age groups. Lack of security has a negative effect on every aspect of their lives: income and consumption, relationships, conjugal stability, family networks, involvement in collective life, and friendship. Their situation grows steadily worse as they move from steady jobs to insecure jobs, and from insecure jobs to short-term and then long-term unemployment. Individuals who were born after 1955, whose suicide rate at the ages between 20 and 40 is much higher than that for their elders, discover, when they begin work, a world that is very different to the one experienced by their elders: no upward mobility, a relative fall in income, mass unemployment, rising rates of poverty. The social content of a whole life stage, namely youth, has, in a word, changed drastically.

The same was true, but in a very different sense, for older people in the 1970s and afterwards. The older generations who, to a greater or lesser extent, enjoyed the cumulative benefits of the previous expansion, were not so violently affected by the reversal of the situation and the sudden emergence of neo-liberal policies. Having experienced full employment throughout their lives, having been taken on on a rising salary basis, having profited from inflation due to home-ownership, they still benefited, upon retirement, from the impetus given to their careers, the generosity of the Welfare State, which guaranteed senior citizens greater protection against economic uncertainties, and the increased life expectancy attributable to advances in medicine. Life expectancy does not increase because a medical cornucopia is administered to a passive population. We live longer not only because we are cared for but mainly because we look after ourselves and because we have looked after ourselves. We no longer sit at the foot of the cherry tree and wait for the basket to fill itself, for the pain in the left side of our chest to stop or for the doctor who was called at the last moment to come too late. Health, too, has become a matter of predicting future needs. And Luc Boltanski's work (1971), which has been confirmed by INSEE's studies of mortality rates, shows that the ability to predict the healthcare we might need is determined by the capital, in particular the cultural capital, at an individual's disposal. The differences between managers and workers has less to do with the symptoms they complain of than in the strategies they use when they consult doctors. Perhaps that is why they enjoy better protection against illness, and also the risk of suicide. Consulting a psychiatrist and foreseeing the risks associated with nervous depression are not behaviours that are equally socially acceptable or expected in the town and in the countryside, in city centres or on suburban estates. When they are acceptable, reasons for committing suicide melt like snow in the sun.

Since the overall restructuring of capitalist economies undertaken during the second half of the 1970s onwards, young people have become more vulnerable and old people more protected. The spectacular change in the age profile of suicide can therefore be related to the in-depth transformation of the social regime for different age groups in France.

There is no French exception . . .

These transformations are not specific to France: in most OECD countries, the last fifty years have been characterized by falling suicide rates amongst old people and rising suicide rates amongst young people from the 1975 crisis onwards. This pattern is in keeping with the model described in detail by Louis Chauvel and emerged for reasons similar to those in France. It applies quite unambiguously to the following countries: Australia, Austria, Belgium, Canada, Denmark, United States, Finland, France, Greece, Italy, Mexico (where the increase mainly affects young people), the Netherlands, New Zealand, Norway, Singapore, Sweden, Switzerland and Great Britain.

The case of Great Britain is especially significant, as this is a country where suicide rates fell throughout this period, with the male rate gradually falling from 13.6 in 1950 to 10.2 in 2000, and with the female rate falling from 7.0 to 3.0. The falling rate for both men and women is largely attributable to the very big drop in suicides amongst older people. The emergence of the category of senior citizens, advances in medicine and the many years of continuous growth helped to improve the lot of old people. Amongst men, on the other hand, the downward trend is in part offset by rising suicide rates amongst young people, especially from 1975 onwards: 5.4 in 1950, 7.8 in 1975, and 10.5 in 2000. The upward trend became more pronounced after 1975, but it was already present during the *Trente Glorieuses*. Young women are less affected by the trend towards greater insecurity. Over the last fifty years, the suicide rate for women aged between 15 and 29 hovered at around 3 per 100,000. The difference in the way men and women react to economic transformations is not specific to Great Britain. We will re-examine this question in the light of other data.

Fig. 6.3 (page 109) provides an almost literal illustration of what Louis Chauvel calls 'the flattening out of suicide rates by age'. Much lower in 1950, the rate for the youngest men caught up with and even

Figure 6.3 Evolution of male suicide rates, Great Britain (1950–2000)

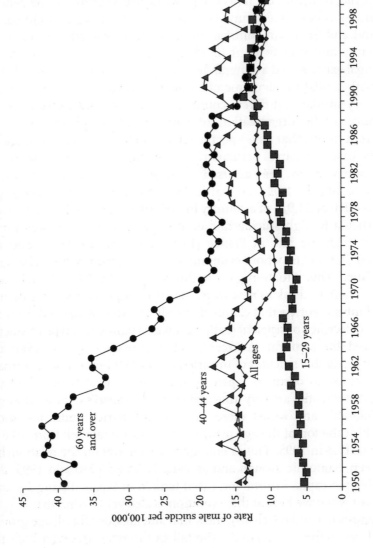

Source: INED.

overtook that for the oldest in 2000. Similar transformations are observable amongst women, albeit not on the same scale.

. . . But there are Japanese and German exceptions

Some rich countries do, however, prove to be exceptions to the general trend. In Federal Germany, suicide rates for all ages declined. In Ireland and Spain, in contrast, the rapid modernization of both the economy and society went hand in hand with a general increase. Portugal experienced a general decrease in rates that were already low in 1950. Whilst the dynamic of change is, in some respects, general and very similar in different countries – increased life expectancy, for instance – the organization of each society is characterized by different trends that have specific effects on the evolution of suicide.

The case of Japan is particularly interesting. The country has often, and quite wrongly, been accused of being a society that is particularly prone to suicide. It is true that in 1950, when it had the modest per capita GDP of $1,921 of a country impoverished by war, Japan did have a particularly high suicide rate of 19.6 per 100,000. This was much higher than the rate in France (15.2), Great Britain (10.2) and the United States (7.6), whose economies were performing much better at the time.[2] This situation gave anthropologists food for thought and forced them to think in new ways. Maurice Pinguet (1984) has demolished the stereotype that claims that ordinary suicide derived from ritualized sacrifice or *seppuku* (better known as *hara-kiri*, a type of suicide reserved for samurai in exceptional circumstances) and even the romantic double suicides of thwarted lovers.[3] Unheroic and unromantic suicides do occur in Japan, recorded only by statistics. And the Japanese statistics are very informative: whilst Japan's wealth increased considerably and whilst there were, as in all rich countries, more people at the top of the age pyramid, the suicide rate fell from 19.6 in 1950 to 17.3 in 1995. This is enough to cast doubt on the relationship between economic growth and suicide: between 1950 and 1995, disposable per capita income increased tenfold in Japan. Taking age into account when we look at this evolution is also very instructive.

Figures 6.3 and 6.4 clearly show that suicide rates for all age groups fell. If we refine the analysis, the fall in the rates amongst both the

---

[2] $5,271 for France, $6,939 for Great Britain and $9,561 for the United States in Geary Khamis 1990 international dollars (see Maddison 2005).

[3] See also the Introduction to this book, 'The contribution of social anthropology'.

Figure 6.4 Male suicide rates by age, Japan, 1950 and 1995

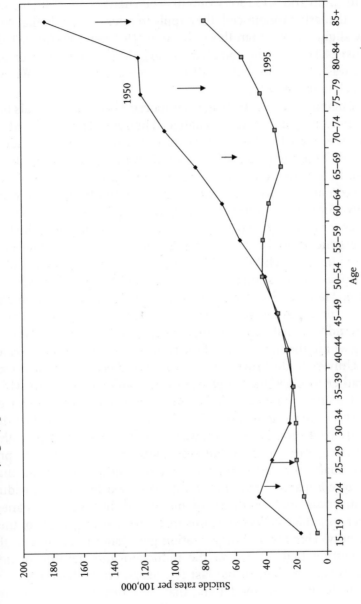

Source: INED.

youngest (−2,414 for men and −2,786 for women) and the oldest (−3,896 for men and −3,427 for women) more than compensated for the rise that should have resulted from the ageing of the population (5,920 for men and 4,133 for women). The changes affecting women were particularly pronounced: they apply to rates of suicide that were initially slightly lower than those for men (15.3 per 100,000 in 1950, as against 24.1) but, at the end of the period, the gap between men and women was similar to that in all the developed countries. We will come back to this point.

Introducing the category of age is important because it reveals how suicide rates respond to social change. The remarkable thing about the Japanese statistics for these years is the decrease in suicide at every level of the age pyramid, and especially the relatively significant decrease in suicide amongst young people during a period of very strong economic growth that put Japan at the forefront of the world economy. The explanation for these figures for suicide is probably that Japan has for a long time taken great care to integrate and induct the younger generation by organizing the novel forms of enterprise capitalism upon which Michio Morishima and Hiroatsu Nohara place such emphasis (Morishima 1987; Maurice and Nohara 1999; see also Lanciano, Maurice, Silvestre and Nohara 1998). Morishima emphasizes the cultural dimensions specific to a Japanese capitalism based in a non-individualistic country that has no puritan tradition. Nohara, working within the framework of the comparative studies undertaken by the Université de Provence's Laboratoire d'économie du travail, tends rather to place the emphasis on the different ways in which different societies organize skills: 'Young Japanese find it relatively easy to enter the world of work. This has less to do with the fact that their early education is geared towards the job market, than with a labour-management system that emphasizes their potential for professional adaptation rather than specific qualifications.' Rather than setting up companies that are strongly oriented towards individual competitiveness and productivity on an ad hoc basis, Japanese employers organize collective teams that have a strong sense of their own identity. This form of organization goes hand in hand with the great attention that is paid to the induction and training of new recruits. We know that, in the last few years, cracks have begun to appear in the Japanese model and that, as a result of globalization, Anglo-American forms of corporate business are introducing flexibility, a lack of security and individualism into Japanese society. Suicide rates faithfully reflect this shift in economic organization: they have

Figure 6.5 Female suicide rates according to age in Japan, 1950 and 1995

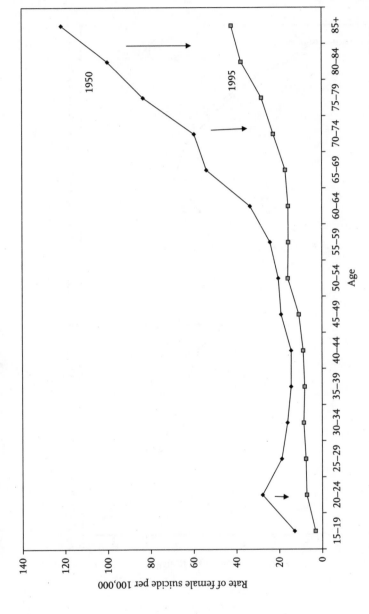

Source: INED.

Figure 6.6 Male suicide rate according to age in Japan, 1995 and 2000

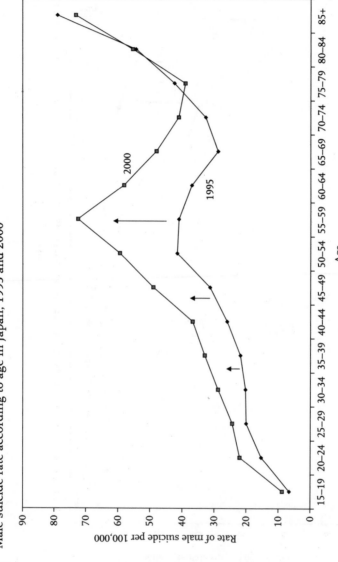

Source: INED.

suddenly risen and have not spared the young. Only the oldest people succeeded in holding their own.

This sudden change was less pronounced amongst women: the male suicide rate rose from 24.3 to 35.2 over a period of five years, whereas that for women rose from 11.3 to 13.4 (see Figs. 6.6 and 6.7, pages 114 and 116).

The case of Japan is instructive. It is the only rich country in which a marked decline in suicide over a period of fifty years has been followed by a sudden rise in the last decade. It shows that suicide rates are extraordinarily sensitive to changes affecting economic and social life and the living and working conditions of the different age groups.

There was no sharp rise in suicide amongst the young in Germany either. Like Japan, Germany saw a significant decline in suicide amongst all age groups. Over the five-year period from 1985 to 1990, the male suicide rate fell from 29.4 per 100,000 to 22.4 in all the western *Länder*. How are we to explain this? Let us attempt to do so in terms similar to those for Japan. An education system with better links between schools and industry makes it easier for young people to enter the world of work; the unemployment rate amongst young Germans is in fact no higher than that for other age groups. Far from acting as a regulatory mechanism, vocational training is highly valued. A German engineer is regarded as a successful worker. Wage and income inequalities are lower in Germany than in either France or the United States. Above all, forms of age segregation are much less pronounced there than in other European countries in terms of wages, employment, access to housing and even inheritance. All these differences define a different economic and social organization of all life stages. And they are reflected in the different age profile for suicide.

The major factors influencing the changes in the age pyramid send us back to sociology itself and to the major transformations undergone by the system and its agents. We cannot simply see age as a transparent variable that can simply be cancelled out in order to standardize comparisons between countries or time periods.

The end of the Italian miracle and British complacency

It is, on the other hand, useful to analyse the specific effects that the same context of economic crisis has on different countries. Whilst all the developed countries experienced a sharp strong downturn in growth during the 1970s, it did not affect the same age groups at the

Figure 6.7 Female suicide rates according to age, Japan, 1995 and 2000

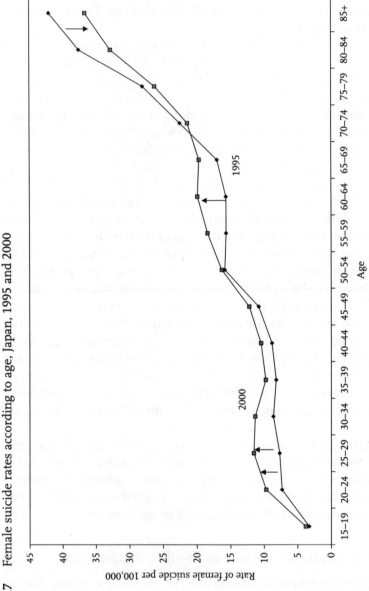

Source: INED.

same time. We can learn a lot from a comparison between Great Britain and Italy, which both have low suicide rates.

Between 1950 and 1975, which was a period of strong growth, the main factors that transformed the pattern of suicide in Great Britain were, in terms of their impact on the total number of suicides:

- a sharp drop in suicides amongst those aged over sixty (−453 suicides);
- a more moderate decrease in suicide rates for those aged between 44 and 60 (−382 suicides);
- a slight increase in suicides amongst young people (+118 suicides);
- the general ageing of the population (+101 suicides).

Between 1975 and 2000, the picture changes considerably:

- the suicide rate for old people falls, but at a slower rate (−271);
- the increased rate for younger people compensates for that fall (+146 for those aged between 15 and 29, and +207 for those between 30 and 44);
- the ageing of the population has only a negligible effect on suicide rates.

1950–1975: these are the twenty-five years favouring senior citizens, who were increasing in number and were better protected. From 1975 onwards, it was the turn of young adults to come first.

The period of the 'Italian miracle' was characterized by a general decline in suicide rates for all ages (−881) that was scarcely affected by the ageing of the population (+201). All generations benefited from the economy's growth, which was not the case in Great Britain. Conversely, only the oldest age groups enjoyed some weak protection after the oil crisis (−68). The oil crisis affected all generations aged between 15 and 60 (+465). And the differences between the rates for different age groups remained big enough for the ageing of the population to lead to a significant rise in the number of suicides (+153).

British growth during the *Trente Glorieuses* did not have the same miraculous effects on this old economic metropolis as on an almost underdeveloped country such as Italy. Conversely, the reversals of fortune were more easily absorbed by the well-off there, whereas all social strata in Italy were put at risk when threatened with the loss of a very recently achieved happy mean. Suicide is therefore influenced by the transformations that social change forces on the different age groups. The intergenerational relations that had been established during the *Trente Glorieuses* were challenged by the downturn in growth. This had the general effect of flattening out suicide rates by age, a process influenced in turn by the characteristics specific to the society in which it took place.

Taking the social dimensions of age seriously

The overall transformation in the pattern of suicide during the last quarter of the twentieth century was spectacular and suggests a need to reflect upon the scale of the upheavals caused in our societies by the new economic climate. In the statistical series published by large public bodies, the scale and meaning of this trend are, however, often masked by the use of the statistically irreproachable technique of presenting 'standardized suicide rates' by arguing on an 'all other things being equal' basis. Suicide rates vary with age and, until very recently, more old people than young people committed suicide. In their comparative series of statistics country-by-country (or statistics for one country over a long time period), epidemiologists and demographers, always keen to be rigorous in their comparisons, try to cancel out the effect of differently structured age pyramids in order to compare, on an 'equal age' basis, actual social realities for countries or regions. A country with a very high proportion of people over 60 is characterized by an unweighted suicide rate that is, *a priori*, higher than that of a neighbouring country where those over 60 occupy a smaller section of the age pyramid. The former country does not necessarily have more suicides than the latter; it simply has more older people, which is a very different matter. In order to cancel out the effect of this ageing and to measure comparable national rates, suicide rates are 'standardized'; they are, in other words, calculated as though the age pyramid was one and the same in both countries. The 'pure differences' between the two countries are then measured by eliminating the differences in the way their populations are ageing. The same technique is applied to historical series within the same country: the age structure of 1950 is, for example, applied to the French population of 2000.

This technique is legitimate if the effect of age is constant in terms of both time and space. It becomes deceptive when major upheavals mean that age has a differential effect on patterns of suicide, as it has done for the last twenty-five years, and when, as we have just seen, those upheavals take different forms in different countries.

Figure 6.8   Male suicide rates according to age, Netherlands, 1950 and 2000

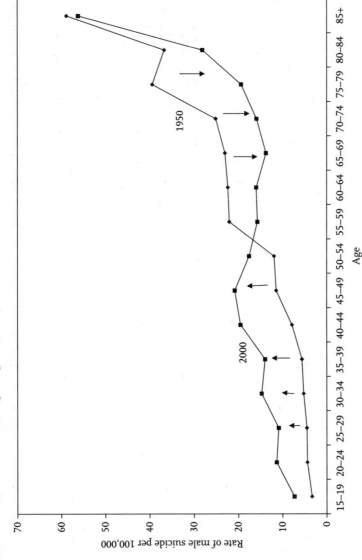

Source: INED.

Figure 6.9 Female suicide rates according to age, Netherlands, 1950 and 2000

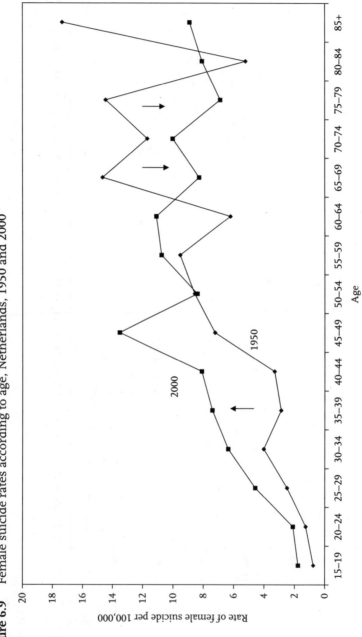

The extent of the changes affecting women reflects the scale used. A variation of 1 in 100,000 in very low female rates can give the illusion of a spectacular leap.
Source: INED.

To prove the point, let us take the concrete example of changes in the suicide rate in the Netherlands between 1950 and 2000. Over a period of fifty years, the male suicide rate rose from 7.4 to 12.7; the female rate also rose from 3.7 to 6.2. If we 'standardize' these rates by applying, for example, the 1950 population structure to the year 2000, we reduce the rate slightly. We have a rate of 10.2 and not 12.7 for men in 2000, and of 5.0 rather than 6.2 for women. We can therefore conclude that much of the increase can be attributed to the ageing of the population. The social reasons for the rest have yet to be explained. However, this standardization approach is extremely reductive in both numerical and conceptual terms. If we take the trouble to analyse the effects in terms of age, we reach a much more instructive conclusion.

Between 1950 and 2000, 341 more male suicides and 168 more female suicides were recorded in the Netherlands.

Less than half of the rise in male suicides (155) is related to changes in the age pyramid. The remaining 186 suicides result from a rising rate for the same age groups. But – and this is the important point – the overall rise of 186 results from lower suicide rates in those aged over fifty years (−103) and a much greater rise in suicides amongst the youngest men (+289).

Precisely the same is true for women: 86 extra suicides can be attributed to the distortion of the age pyramid, and 82 to the overall rise in the suicide rate. The same dissymmetry applies as for men: there were fewer suicides amongst the eldest (−18) and many more (+100) amongst the youngest.[4] Apart from the predictable effects of changes in the age pyramid, there were no obvious social transformations affecting the level of suicide in the Netherlands between 1950 and 2000. The social transformations were mainly to do with changes in the status of different age groups, as can be clearly seen in Figures 6.8 and 6.9 (pages 119 and 120).

Such is the new pattern of suicide by age. There is no reason to believe that it will enjoy the same longevity as the old model, which lasted for over one hundred and fifty years. The uncertainty surrounding pension schemes in most countries, the need to work for longer and above all the fact that it is increasingly difficult for a growing number of workers, who are entering the job market later and later, to work the number of years needed to qualify for a full pension,

---

[4] This estimate is based upon a calculation of the partial derivatives that make it possible to isolate the respective effects of the ageing of the population and changes in the suicide rates by age.

all pose long-term threats to the status of senior citizens, who may, in the near future, experience the end of golden age. Long statistical series show that the one and a half centuries during which suicide rates and age rose is by no means a yardstick for the future. The rapidity and suddenness of economic and social changes suggest, on the contrary, that the present relationship between age and suicide is a very temporary moment in a story that still beats to the rhythm of the life of society.

7 Suicide and Social Class: An Overview

Inequality in the face of death is a tragic indicator of the inequalities of life in society. In contemporary France, those sections of society that live longest enjoy over nine more years of life on earth than those that die youngest. Between these two extremes, life expectancy decreases regularly and steeply as we move down the social ladder. In the period 1980–1990, a worker was twice as likely to die between the ages of 35 and 65 as a senior manager (26% as opposed to 13%). The gap has grown since the 1960s, as the probability of dying between the ages of 35 and 65 fell less amongst social groups where the mortality rate was already higher than in groups where it was lowest. The probability fell by 26% amongst teachers, who were already highly protected, but by only 9.5% amongst unskilled labourers (Desplanques 1993; Surault 1995b; Mesrine 1999; Jougla et al. 2000). In today's France, the social distribution of suicide follows the trends for life expectancy and general mortality identified by demographers. Those social groups whose life expectancy is shortest are also the social groups that are most at risk of suicide. Suicide now strikes in those areas where life is most uncertain, most at risk, harshest and shortest. This has not always been the case.

In order to arrive at a clear picture of the relationship between social milieus and suicide today, we will adopt two successive viewpoints. The first is based on regional statistics gathered in three rich countries: the United States, France and Great Britain. They demonstrate that, in all three countries, there is a clear fall in the suicide rate as we move from the poorest to the richest regions, be they states (the United States), départements (France) or districts (Great Britain). The second viewpoint, which is more individual and focuses on France, analyses the distribution of suicide in terms of social categories and professions. The findings of both analyses are similar: suicide is most common in the poorest and most disadvantaged regions and social categories. There is a striking contrast between the picture at the end of the twentieth century and the situation analysed by Durkheim in the nineteenth.

The American geography of suicide

In the United States, the suicide rate is lowest in the richest and most modern states (California, Illinois, New Jersey). The states where it is highest are those whose poverty and geographical situation mean that they are very distant from the centres of the 'American way of life' (see Fig. 7.1, page 125).

By using very detailed statistics based on counties (administrative subdivisions of states), some researchers (Cutler, Glaeser and Norberg 2004) have calculated that the suicide rate falls by 1.4% as median incomes diverge from a standard disparity. Diachronic statistics state by state demonstrate that the protection afforded by wealth has increased between 1950 and today.

The French *départements*: income tax and suicide

The same can be done for contemporary France. Wealth is unevenly distributed across France's *départements* and, as in the United States, poverty is associated with a certain level of marginalization in all areas of social life: stagnant demography, distance from big urban centres, inadequate educational resources. The percentage of households with taxable incomes provides a good measure of the relative wealth of different *départements*. A link can therefore be established between suicide and wealth. Suicide rates are lowest in the richest, most modern and most urbanized *départements*. The poorest *départements* hold the record for the highest number of suicides.[1]

We can begin by identifying a group of 12 *départements* with a very low suicide rate of between 5.9 and 19.5 per 100,000: Paris, Seine-Saint-Denis, Val-de-Marne, Moselle, Haute-Garonne, Hauts-de-Seine, Rhône, Bas-Rhin, Alpes-Maritimes, Yvelines, Val-d'Oise and Essonne. This is a group of *départements* where a high proportion of the population (61%) pays income tax and where only a small (11%) proportion of the population is over 60 years old.

---

[1] The following four categories are based on male suicide rates for 2000–1; these are higher and more widespread than the female rates. The correlation between male and female rates is, however, almost perfect.

Figure 7.1 Suicide rates by income, USA (2001)

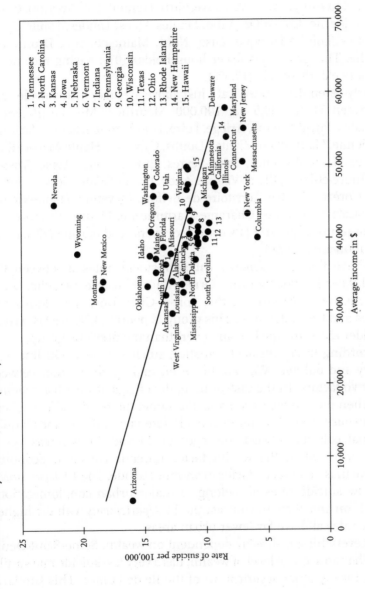

Source: Glen Evans, Norman Farberow, *The Encyclopedia of Suicide*, New York, 2003.

Then we have a group of 33 *départements* with suicide rates that are slightly below the average (between 20.6 and 30.7 per 100,000): Seine-et-Marne, Jura, Haut-Rhin, Isère, Bouches-du-Rhône, Tarn-et-Garonne, Lozère, Savoie, Ain, Gironde, Pyrenées-Atlantiques, Gard, Haute-Savoie, Hautes-Pyrenées, Vaucluse, Tarn, Hérault, Lot, Aveyron, Corse-du-Sud, Marne, Côte-d'Or, Aube, Hautes-Alpes, Landes, Haute-Corse, Ardennes, Loire-Atlantique, Oise, Nord, Maine-et-Loire, Drôme and Ardèche. This group has fewer households (50%) paying income tax and more elderly people (19.5%).

Thirty-seven *départements* are just above average, with suicide rates of between 31 and 39.5 per 100,000: Meurthe-et-Moselle, Pyrénées-Orientales, Puy-de-Dôme, Ariège, Loire, Loiret, Yonne, Seine-Maritime, Var, Vienne, Haute-Loire, Cantal, Doubs, Calvados, Haute-Marne, Eure, Alpes-de-Haute-Provence, Deux-Sèvres, Eure-et-Loire, Aisne, Vosges, Cher, Indre-et-Loire, Ille-et-Vilaine, Aude, Haute-Saône, Gers, Saône-et-Loire, Corèze, Vendée, Territoire de Belfort, Mayenne, Haute-Vienne, Pas-de-Calais, Charente, Charente-Maritime and Meuse. We move up a rung in terms of poverty (48% are tax payers) and old age (27% of the population are over 60).

We have, finally, 14 *départements* with suicide rates of between 39.8 and 51.9 per 100,000: Somme, Orne, Allier, Finistère, Manche, Lot-et-Garonne, Indre, Creuse, Sarthe, Loir-et-Cher, Dordogne, Morbihan, Nièvres and Côtes-d'Armor. This group is poorer (47% are tax payers) and older (27% are aged 60 and over) than the previous group.

According to *département* statistics, suicide rates are in line with poverty and old age. We can, however, make a distinction between these two factors. In the case of men, the effects of wealth are significant when the age factor remains the same: the relationship between a *département's* wealth and its suicide rate is significant for all quinquennial cohorts between the ages of 20 and 70, whereas age is insignificant when the wealth factor remains constant. Economic dynamism is no longer a factor in anomic suicide. The 12 *départements* with low suicide rates all belong to major urban conglomerations: Paris, Lyon and Nice. In contrast the 14 *départements* with the highest suicide rates all have far fewer urban areas.

Not everything is directly dependent on wealth. Seine-Saint-Denis, which has an average level of wealth, has a very low suicide rate similar to that for the other *départements* of the Ile-de-France. This similarity is probably due to the indirect effect of the affluence of the Paris region as a whole: urbanization. And this is another paradox, given that there is so much negative talk about the big city environment, the social dis-

Map 7.1   Proportion of households paying income tax by *département* (2000–2001)

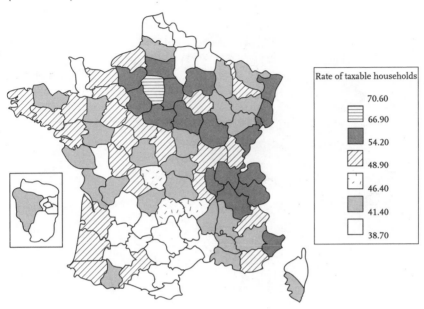

Rate of taxable households

70.60

66.90

54.20

48.90

46.40

41.40

38.70

Source: INED.

integration that is supposedly taking place there, and so on. We can also see that across the board, given a constant level of affluence, suicide rates are lower in the *départements* of the south than in those of the north. But whilst wealth does not explain everything and whilst its effects are felt only via some of its distant social consequences, it is undeniable that it does have an impact upon suicide. The rich are spared and the poor are at risk. If we compare the two maps (suicide rates by *département* and the proportion of households paying income tax), this fact is quite unambiguous.

The map of suicide at the end of the twentieth century is, in almost every respect, the very opposite of that compiled by Durkheim for the years 1878–87 (Durkheim 1897: Map 7.2).

The urban *départements* that once had the highest suicide rates now have the lowest. This change is especially remarkable in the case of all the *départements* of the Ile-de-France, which once headed the list and now come last. The same thing has happened in Bouches-du-Rhône, Rhône, Alpes-Maritimes and, to a lesser degree, Gironde and Isère. In all these cases, there has been not only a change of position but also a substantial decline in suicide rates.

Map 7.2   Distribution of rates of suicide by *département* (2000–2001)

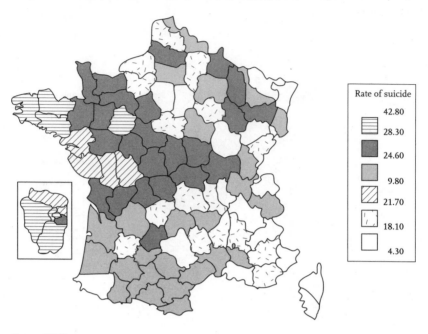

Rate of suicide	
	42.80
▤	28.30
▨	24.60
▦	9.80
▨	21.70
☐	18.10
☐	4.30

Source: INED.

In contrast, the rural *départements* of western France, which once had the lowest suicide rates, now have the highest. This is true of all the *départements* in Brittany and for Manche, Calvados, Indre, Charente, Charente-Maritime, Sarthe and Indre. It is also true of many *départements* in the Massif Central (Haute-Vienne, Creuse, Corrèze, Allier, Ardèche and Nièvre) and of the rural *départements* in eastern France (Marne, Haute-Marne, Meuse and Ardennes) and in the north (Somme). This is not just a matter of a change of position; there has been a very substantial rise in the suicide rate.

It is clear that this evolution has been to the advantage of urban centres. It should also be noted that Loire-Atlantique is the only *département* in western France to have experienced a positive evolution. This is also true of the Loire *département* in the Massif Central, of Seine-Maritime and Eure in Normandy, and of Meurthe-et-Moselle in the east. The position of the Nord *département* has improved, unlike that of Pas-de-Calais and especially Somme. The beneficial effect of the big cities – Nantes, Nancy, Lille, Le Havre and Saint-Etienne – was felt very clearly in the twentieth century.

In the nineteenth century, suicide rates seemed to rise in line with development, wealth and urbanization. In the twentieth, the opposite was true. The greater the influence of a county town [chef-lieu] on a département, the lower its suicide rate. And it is the fully urbanized départements of the Paris region that have the lowest rates. Suicide rates vary greatly in inverse proportion to population density (-0.47). The Paris region obviously has a great influence on this correlation. But if we look only at the provincial départements, it is still significant (20.28). But is urbanization the reason? Or is it the affluence that is closely correlated with it?

INSEE has used all the available data to construct a discriminant typology of all France's départements (Hilico and Didier 2004). The chart that emerges can be compared with that for suicide.

The Ile-de-France, together with the three départements associated with it, differs from all other regions in several respects: urbanization, the economic activity of women, a high proportion of managerial staff, major companies, a high level of affluence, high life expectancy, good medical cover, high numbers of students in higher education. This region, in particular its centre (Paris, Seine-Saint-Denis, Val-de-Marne), is characterized by its extremely low suicide rate. However, one hundred years ago, all these départements had the highest suicide rates.

All the Mediterranean départements, from the Pyrénées-Orientales to the Alpes-Maritimes, have, without exception, been transformed by tourism. They have high levels of medical cover and large active populations in the retail and administrative sectors. It is the second region where suicide rates have fallen since the nineteenth century. The fall is less marked than in Paris, but it is still real. Suicide rates are lowest in the most densely populated and most highly urbanized départements, namely Bouches-du-Rhône and Alpes-Maritimes (15.4 and 15.2, respectively).

In contrast, two groups of regions have experienced a rise in the suicide rate. They are the 'rural industrial' départements of western France, which are characterized by the dominance of industry, industrial workers and occupations that are traditionally male, and a definite deficit in the tertiary sector. Their suicide rates of between 22.3 (Deux-Sèvres) and 42.8 (Côtes-d'Armor) are far above the national average. In the nineteenth century, they were amongst the lowest. It should again be noted that the most urbanized département (Loire-Atlantique) has the lowest suicide rate: 22.9.

The rural départements of the south-west share many of these socio-economic characteristics, but they are less affluent and have older populations. All these *départements* have experienced a moderate increase in suicides, which is greater in the rural *départements* of the southern Massif Central. Haute-Garonne, along with Toulouse, clearly stands out from the region as a whole: its suicide rate is only 9.8, whereas it is between 18 and 26% (Lot, Charente-Maritime) in the region as a whole.

There has been no change in two regions: the industrial *départements* of the north, which had high suicide rates in the nineteenth century. Once again, it is the most urbanized *département* that has, in relative terms, the lowest suicide rate: Nord (20.0). The effects of the upheavals of the nineteenth century (the industrial revolution) and the twentieth (de-industrialization) have been the same.

The *départements* around Lyon (Rhône, Isère, Drôme, Loire and Puy-de-Dôme) are in the same bracket as they were in the nineteenth century. Once again, the most urbanized *département* has the lowest suicide rate (Rhône: 13.3). Rates remain stable in the most active *départements* (Isère and Drôme), whilst the two *départements* that have experienced a certain downturn (Loire and Puy-de-Dôme) have recorded a slight increase in suicides.

In the nineteenth century, modernity led to suicide; it affected the most dynamic regions and protected the most backward. In the twentieth century, modernity was a protective factor. But is it possible to identify the individual components of the social factors that influence the risk of suicide? Is it a matter of affluence? Of the degree of medical cover? Or is it simply an effect of density itself, and of all the various things on offer that can sustain the will to live? Or is it due to interesting jobs that can be a source of personal happiness?

Separating out these factors is no doubt a fanciful undertaking. But when confronted with the problem of the risk of suicide, it is perhaps not very reasonable. There is no doubt a complex interaction between those elements within modernity that can give a meaning to life and provide solutions for our anxieties. We would do well to recall the lesson Maurice Halbwachs learned from his attempt to distinguish (1930: 189), in his discussion of suicidogenic factors, between the effects of religion and those of professional life:

> It is difficult indeed to distinguish religious habits from other customs, as most often they form a whole which cannot be resolved into constituent parts. Is the peasant attached to his church because this is the location of the cult, or because to him it represents his village? Does he honour his dead and maintain their graves because he thinks of the community of the living and the dead, of the future life, or because he preserves the

remembrance of those who have preceded him, in his house and on his land, and through traditional attachment to what represents the past? Does suicide horrify him because it is an unpardonable sin or because whoever kills himself is deemed peculiar and dies according to forms which are inadmissible in the rural community? To be able to distinguish what is and what is not truly religious, the religious group must not be intermingled with a non-religious society; its rites and ceremonies must not at all be bound up with traditional customs and festivals that are without any transcendental meaning.

What this little *tour de France* teaches us is that modern society, with all its interactive dimensions, greatly reduces the risk of suicide. Conversely, those regions and milieus that struggle to live by contemporary standards are most at risk. Our *tour de France* was worthwhile because it challenges more than one common view of the inhuman nature of the modern city.

Ken Loach's devastated England versus Blair–Thatcher's Greater London

British statistics provide further confirmation that there is a link between poverty and suicide in the developed countries. Here again, the inclusion of 'occupation' in the 'cause of death' category leaves us in no doubt: suicide is more common in the most disadvantaged categories. The regional statistics allow us to go beyond the fiscal data for France. British demographers have looked at various forms of social deprivation by taking into account six basic measures. Peter Townsend, for example, develops (1970) the concept of deprivation on the basis of several indicators, including lack of material well-being or of possible involvement in social life (income, employment, health and handicaps, education and skills, housing and geographical accessibility).

The statistics take poverty into account when considering these six indicators for each district or ward. Each district can then be defined according to a scale of deprivation. Once more, there is no doubt about the diagnosis: the risk of suicide is greatest in those districts that have the most shortcomings. If we take the male suicide rate for a given age group, we find that it is closely correlated with low income (-0.05) and even more closely with unemployment (-0.57). Synthetic statistics that take account of all dimensions of social deprivation reveal, however, an even closer correlation (-0.76 for the synthetic index of multiple disadvantages concentrated within a given district). Districts such as Birmingham and Manchester, which rank highest in terms of the concentration of social deprivation, have the highest suicide rates. Britain seems to be traversed by a Centre–North/West–London axis, which might also be called the Ken Loach/Blair–Thatcher axis. All the major towns that have been devastated by de-industrialization in the central north-west are in the red in terms of both suicide and overall social deprivation: Bolton (a former textile town), Preston, Liverpool, Wirral (near Liverpool), Manchester, Barrow-in-Furness (near Copeland), Pendle (a former textile town forty-five minutes away from Manchester) and Lancaster. The only London borough to figure in this category is Lambeth, a blighted area in which 40% of the population is of immigrant origin. Most parts of Greater London and all the outlying residential suburbs of Kent, Essex and southern Northamptonshire (Kelly and Bunting 1998) are on the other side of the dividing line and have very low suicide rates.

Suicide and social milieu in France

The data on the social position and occupation of individual suicide victims makes it possible to explore the links between wealth and suicide in greater detail. These data, whose availability varies from country to country, are not without their imperfections, as it is always more difficult to establish the occupation of someone who is dead than that of someone who is alive. Forensic medical examiners and police officers are not census takers. The primary concern of the doctors, police officers or *gendarmes* who collect the information given on death certificates is to determine that the cause of death really was suicide and not murder or an accident. The sociological need to record accurately a suicide's last known occupation is the least of their concerns. Hence, no doubt, the high number of 'employees' amongst today's suicides: the label is often applied for want of anything better when there is no more concrete indication as to the victim's last known occupation.

Whilst there is a large margin of error when it comes to classifying the statistics for suicide in terms of social categories, they are reliable provided that we consider them over time and do not over-interpret them. Since the end of the Second World War, several broad tendencies have become apparent: there are more – many more – suicides at the bottom of the social hierarchy than at the top. And yet it is not always the same social groups that have the highest suicide rates: agricultural workers, workers and employees have all had the highest rates, depending on the period and the economic situation. Occupational differences are more pronounced amongst men than amongst women. The discrepancies between the different social groups are, in all cases, so great and so consistent that we can, at this high level of generality, overlook the inadequacies of the statistical record.

Nicolas Bourgoin (1999), a demographer at INED, provides a picture of France in the period 1984–94. Using relevant data collected over the last thirty years, he analyses the link between unemployment and suicide on the one hand, and suicide and socio-professional categories on the other. The interest of this study lies in the details of the variations observed. The author attempts to differentiate between periods, gender and age groups.

One thing is certain: those who are economically active are much less likely to commit suicide than those who are inactive: the 'inactive' category includes the unemployed – irrespective of whether or not they have ever worked – housewives, those who were formerly in active work, those who took early retirement at 55 or above, the disabled and those in receipt of *Revenu Minimum d'Insertion*. The ratio between suicide rates for the economically inactive and the active is not, however, stable, and varies over time. In 1978, inactive men aged between 25 and 59 committed suicide three and a half times more often than men who were actively occupied. The ratio was even higher in 1992 (2.3 times more often), but it then fell after reaching its lowest (1.8) in 1982. For women, in contrast, the ratio was lower but rose over time (from 1.3 to 1.9). These variations suggest that it is not so much inactivity as such that encourages suicide as the social and psychological conditions that are associated with it and the way in which they are experienced. The relative decline recorded for men may be attributable to a greater degree of acceptance of unemployment over time, whilst the rise in suicides amongst women may indicate a change in their professional aspirations: they may have a greater tendency to experience unemployment as a failure at a time when, as female rates of activity rose, the model of the active, professional woman became accepted as the norm.

There is nothing universal about the link between unemployment and suicide. Its existence has not been demonstrated in three neighbouring countries – Italy, Germany and Great Britain – where unemployment rates rose without any corresponding rise in suicide rates. Nor has it been shown to exist in the case of France, at least not at a general level. Whilst the correlation is not significant in overall terms, the link displays great variations depending on age and gender. The highly significant link between unemployment and suicide is most pronounced amongst men under 25, and in particular amongst men aged between 25 and 49. It is, on the other hand, almost non-existent amongst women and amongst men over 50, even though they are the most likely to commit suicide. The sharp rise in unemployment in France from 1999 onwards did not lead to an upsurge in suicide in men over 50, but it did so in the case of younger men.

The ordeal of unemployment is therefore very traumatic for young men, as it denies them access to a source of values and the focus provided by work which, quite apart from giving them a regular income, confers status, recognition, a feeling of being useful and of being recognized as useful, an opportunity to make friends and enemies, a disciplined use of time and space, and the ability to plan for the future. The shock is not as harsh for older men, who have been able to accumulate experience and social status and who are close to receiving a generous pension, which usually comes at a time when they are just coming into their inheritance. The material and moral support families still give to children under 25 also explains why the link is strongest between the ages of 25 and 49; after the age of 25, individuals are expected to fight their own battles in the job market. The example of unemployment clearly indicates that there is nothing automatic about the economic situation's impact on suicide rates. It depends mainly on the social, affective and psychological context in which different individuals live, their room for manoeuvre, the support networks to which they belong, the support they enjoy and, more generally, the role and status of work in their lives. The sociologist Serge Paugam's study of the basic forms of poverty (Paugam 2005) allows us to understand these differences, and we will come back to it. The degree to which unemployment encourages or discourages suicide depends on whether work represents a means of salvation or just a way of making a living.

Things are much clearer if we examine the risk of suicide in the light of individuals' social status and occupations. In the case of men, the risks are now very unevenly divided between three main occupational groups, whereas social disparities between women are less pronounced and inequality in the face of suicide is less closely related to social status. Those most at risk are office workers (around 60 per 100,000), and those least at risk are men employed in management, intermediate professions, and the intellectual and liberal professions (20 per 100,000 and below). Between these two groups is one that includes farm workers, factory workers, craftsmen and tradespeople (around 40 per 100,000). The much higher rate of suicide amongst office workers is deceptive. It is in part due to the statistical vagueness of this social category, which includes many individuals of 'unknown occupation', or in other words cases in which there is not enough information to determine the individual's occupation with any certainty. We can hypothetically suggest that, if these uncertainties are discounted, the suicide rate for the 'office workers' category would be similar to that for the group of agricultural workers, factory workers, craftsmen and tradespeople, and there would not necessarily be any great difference between it and other categories.

The social hierarchy that emerges is similar to that for earlier periods in terms of the constant level of protection apparently enjoyed by higher social categories since the Second World War. As in the past, intellectuals, managers and the liberal professions are still the social categories with the fewest number of suicides. The categories that are most at risk are, however, no longer the same. Once again, things are changing.

'In the period 1968–78,' writes Nicolas Bourgoin (1999), 'the occupational group that was most at risk was that of agricultural labourers followed, in order, by office workers, industrial workers, shop and factory owners, the liberal professions and senior management.' In the 1960s, in contrast, it was workers who were most at risk. The profound transformations that had turned the rural world upside down and led to what Henri Mendras (1962) calls 'the end of the peasants' explain the helplessness of the millions of peasants who were forced to leave their land and to sell their labour in the towns. The disappearance of the least productive farms and modernization transformed the picture, and the changes observed in the suicide rate confirm those we note when we look at academic success. Once the conversion of the peasants was complete, the highest suicide rate was found amongst workers. The collapse of the 'working class' in an economic context of de-industrialization and relocation has resulted in the devaluation of labour, the weakening of collective resistance, a crisis in trade union activism and rising racial tensions against a background of mass unemployment. All these trends lead to increased vulnerability (Beaud and Pialoux 1999).

No matter which category heads the league table, one thing is clear (Figs. 7.2 and 7.3).[2] Suicide is now (in the second half of the twentieth

---

[2] It should be noted that the gaps between the extremes are more pronounced amongst men than amongst women.

century and at the beginning of the twenty-first) more common in those social categories at the bottom of the scale. 'The hierarchy of unhappiness is indeed the negative of the hierarchy of social status' (Chesnais 1973). The evolution of suicide and its increase amongst the most disadvantaged categories can, according to Pierre Surault (1991; 1997), be seen as a sign of the drift towards 'a dual society characterized by the emergence of a stratum of those who are excluded – from work, consumption, housing, leisure, holidays and the Internet – and who are reproduced generation after generation without any hope of upward social mobility.'

Nicolas Bourgoin's careful breakdown (1997) of the figures by occupation suggests, however, that these findings require some qualification. A detailed examination confirms that there is a hierarchical tendency: unskilled workers commit suicide more often than skilled workers, primary school teachers more often than secondary school teachers, and rank and file police officers more often than police inspectors. In the police force, the suicide rate for uniformed officers is comparable to that for workers; that for inspectors is similar to that for senior managers. If we turn to the intermediate professions, suicide is most common amongst primary school teachers, whilst among people in supervisory and managerial positions the liberal and artistic professions are much more prone to suicide. If we consider the working classes, office workers are in the lead; in the private and public sectors, it is unskilled workers and shop workers who are most at risk. Conversely, certain occupations within this group, which is on the whole at greater risk, come off better: skilled workers in warehousing, transport and storage depots, foremen and charge hands. All these differences confirm that the world of industrial and office workers is, in social terms, extremely heterogeneous (Chenu 1990).

This heterogeneity has become even more marked over the last forty years as work has become the norm for women. Now that most couples both work, the form of the association between the occupations of men and women has become a major part of class relations, especially in areas such as suicide, where causality has to be sought equally in the work environment as well as in living conditions and the domain of the family. Whilst most marriages do take place within the same social class, there can be significant class differences between partners. If we look at the situation for women, the 'office workers' category is by far the most widespread in terms of the levels of society it reaches (Baudelot and Establet 2005). Women office workers are rarely married to other office workers (15.1%); they

Figure 7.2   Male suicide rates between the ages of 25 and 49 by occupation (1989–1994) (rate per 100,000)

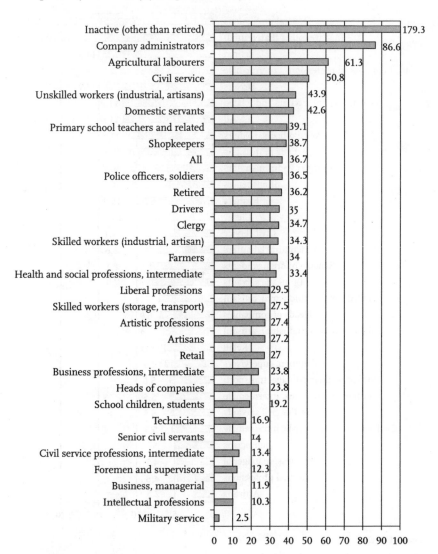

Occupation	Rate
Inactive (other than retired)	179.3
Company administrators	86.6
Agricultural labourers	61.3
Civil service	50.8
Unskilled workers (industrial, artisans)	43.9
Domestic servants	42.6
Primary school teachers and related	39.1
Shopkeepers	38.7
All	36.7
Police officers, soldiers	36.5
Retired	36.2
Drivers	35
Clergy	34.7
Skilled workers (industrial, artisan)	34.3
Farmers	34
Health and social professions, intermediate	33.4
Liberal professions	29.5
Skilled workers (storage, transport)	27.5
Artistic professions	27.4
Artisans	27.2
Retail	27
Business professions, intermediate	23.8
Heads of companies	23.8
School children, students	19.2
Technicians	16.9
Senior civil servants	14
Civil service professions, intermediate	13.4
Foremen and supervisors	12.3
Business, managerial	11.9
Intellectual professions	10.3
Military service	2.5

Source: INED.

usually live with industrial workers (43.3%), but also with managers (31.8%) and sometimes even with men who are self-employed (9.7%).

Women in the liberal and intermediate professions in the health and social sectors have the highest rates of suicide. Most studies find that doctors, nurses and other members of the caring professions have

Figure 7.3   Female suicide rates between the ages of 25 and 49 by occupation (1989–1994) (rate per 100,000)

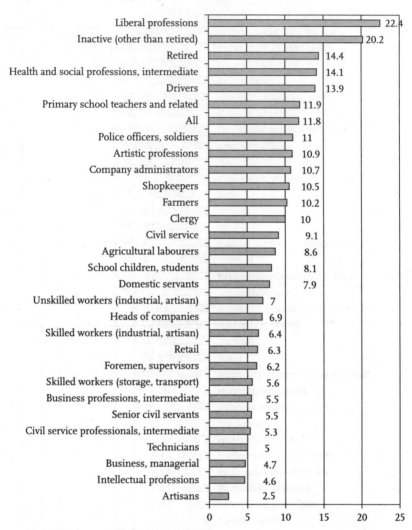

Source: INED.

the highest rates. Their day-to-day familiarity with suffering and death are no doubt relevant here. Most studies of the 'burn out' phenomenon identified in 1980 by the American psychoanalyst Herbert J. Freudenberger (1980) are concerned with nurses working in palliative care units. This syndrome of professional exhaustion presents as sudden inner turmoil when the victims of this occupational disease suffer mental and nervous exhaustion as a result of trying to reach unattainable aims or to perform impossible tasks. The battle against death is obviously one of these tasks.

In order to explain the high suicide rate amongst women in the higher professions, Nicolas Bourgoin notes correctly (1999) that the proportion of single women rises as we go up the social hierarchy, whilst the proportion of men declines. And, as we have known since the late nineteenth century, suicide rates are always higher for single people than for married people. This is true of all ages and of both sexes. We also know that marriage is a professional handicap for women and an advantage for men. If, however, we consider the working classes, 'for women, being well integrated into a family often compensates for work that is socially undervalued, whereas it tends to represent a handicap for men' (Bourgoin 1999). Office and industrial workers and agricultural labourers also have the highest rates of celibacy.

An occupation, like a given level of income, cannot in itself be a factor in suicide, and still less can it be a cause of suicide. In social terms, it is no more than a synthetic indicator of a standard of living and way of life. That is why other dimensions, such as income or educational qualifications, must also be taken into account. Nicolas Bourgoin demonstrates that there is a negative and significant correlation between levels of education and income and male suicide rates. The higher their level of education and/or education, the fewer suicides there are amongst men. These three indicators (occupation, income and qualifications) are by no means the only components that define both milieu and social status. Their convergence nonetheless suggests that the economic and social factors that influence suicide are to be found in the social value attributed to individuals both by society and by themselves.

8 The Twentieth Century: Greater Protection for the Ruling Classes

Has suicide always affected the poorest members of society and spared the more affluent? Nothing could be less certain. We know what Durkheim's answer is. He was led to conclude that suicide was more common at the top of the social hierarchy and that 'poverty protects' the most disadvantaged. He reached this conclusion because he probably read the incomplete statistics of his day too quickly. This point of view has been sharply criticized by Jean-Claude Chesnais (1981), who puts forward an argument that is difficult to refute. In the nineteenth century, the suicide rate rose in spectacular fashion all over France, especially in the big cities and in Paris. Can this strong upward trend be explained solely in terms of the increase in suicides amongst the higher social categories, which were, in numerical terms, very small at the time? Chesnais criticizes Durkheim for having ignored the line recording the highest suicide rates for both men and women in the table published by the *Statistique générale de la France* for the years 1861–65. According to Chesnais, the 'unemployed or occupation unknown' category includes 'the mad, the unemployed, criminals, vagabonds, prostitutes and "disreputables" of all kinds', and domestic servants, or in other words, the marginals whom Victor Hugo called *les misérables* and whom Sébastien Mercier described as being very prone to suicide in his *Tableau de Paris* of 1788. Several similar indicators lead us to conclude that, in nineteenth-century Europe, suicides occurred at both the top and the bottom of the social pyramid. The data collected by Morselli in Italy indicated that suicide was most common amongst the educated classes. Shopkeepers, people living on private incomes, doctors and lawyers often took their own lives, as did teachers and civil servants. The same was true of Prussia, where the civil service, which represented a select elite, was evidently the social group

with the highest suicide rate. 'This "hypersuicidity" amongst intellectuals' was, according to Chesnais, a constant in nineteenth-century
Europe.

Higher-quality sources from Great Britain and the United States
dealing with the late nineteenth century and the first half of the twentieth confirm this diagnosis. There were many suicides at the two
extreme poles of society, but these became fewer in number as we
reach the second half of the twentieth century.

Four sources that have been particularly well exploited are worth
examining in a chronological perspective. It is to be regretted that
studies of this kind have not been made of France or of other European
countries. Although the historical trends that emerge from these
studies apply mainly to the United States, they appear to apply to
France too, as suicide in America is, although on a smaller scale,
subject to the same variations as suicide in France and, more generally, Europe at this time: more men than women, more old people than
young, fewer married people than single or widowed people, more suicides on Mondays and fewer on Sundays, and more during periods of
depression than during periods of growth.

The first study, which we have already cited (Anderson 1987), is
by a historian and deals with Victorian and Edwardian England.
According to the detailed data Olive Anderson has extracted (1987:
70–71) from the archives of the General Register Office for the end of
the nineteenth century and from the returns of three London coroners
in Sussex,[1] six occupations had suicide rates that were over twice the
national average for active men aged between 25 and 44. Half
were working-class occupations – soldiers serving in cavalry regi-
ments and the British Army in India, waiters and guards – whereas
the other three, in contrast, concerned the most highly educated
section of society: doctors, pharmacists and lawyers. Suicide enjoyed
a fairly positive reputation amongst the wealthy at this time: it was
regarded as a sign of freedom, courage and dignity, or even aesthetic
detachment. Amongst the working classes, in contrast, it was the
object of strong disapproval. It was associated with madness and criticized as a cowardly act that destroyed the solidarity of the family. An

---

[1] Until the Suicide Act of 1961, suicide was regarded as a crime (*felonia de se*)
in England. Both the victim's parents and children were liable to prosecution.
During the reign of Victoria, every case in London implied the involvement of at
least thirty to thirty-five people, including police officers, registrars, coroners,
juries, etc.

individual who committed suicide dishonoured him or herself and brought misfortune on his or her family.[2] In the countryside, the disapproval was even greater.

Rich and detailed data from the USA

A second source dealing with the British and American data for the first half of the twentieth century derives from the statistical studies of the famous American actuary Louis Dublin (Dublin and Bunzel 1933), who became Vice-President of the Metropolitan Life Insurance Company (better known as Metlife, and famous for its great building in Manhattan). Having undertaken many studies of public health and mortality rates on behalf of the insurance company, Dublin, working in collaboration with Bessie Bunzel, published a major study of suicide in 1933. In it, he explores in detail the effects of the economic situation on the phenomenon, using the data on clients collected by his own company and surveys carried out in Great Britain for the period 1921–23. The links he establishes between rates of growth and suicide are close, and quite in keeping with the trends observed in Europe. The suicide rate falls when economic activity picks up, and rises during periods of depression. Between 1910 and 1913, when business trends were stable, the suicide rate was always lower than normal. In mid-1913, a depression loomed during the Wilson presidency, and the suicide rate rose rapidly, peaking between 1914 and 1915. It then fell again quite quickly in 1916. The boom in heavy industry resulting from America's entry into the war kept suicide rates low until 1918. The armistice destabilized business and put an end to production in the war industries. Suicide rates rose. With the return of prosperity, they fell from 1919–20 onwards. On the other hand, they began to rise as the economy collapsed after the crisis of 1929.

As for the distribution of suicide across different social groups, Louis Dublin's findings contradict the widespread contemporary view that suicide was more common in the higher strata of society ('among those who have every financial facility to enjoy life than among those who have barely enough money to hold body and soul together'). He

---

[2] The popular idea of suicide was very similar to that expressed by John Netten Radcliffe, a young epidemiologist and cholera specialist during the Crimean War, and the assistant editor of the *Journal of Psychological Medicine*. In a study of suicide in England in the years 1852–56, he attributed it to 'a peculiar vicious or morbid tone of thought' (cited in Anderson 1987: 77).

reveals the existence of two spikes: one at the top of the social scale (capitalists, company bosses, managers and primary school teachers) and one at the bottom (small shopkeepers, clerks in the banking and insurance industries, unskilled workers and tramps). A number of professions were characterized by particularly high suicide rates: the medical professions (doctors and dentists), lawyers and auctioneers, wholesalers and commercial travellers. In other words, suicide was at this time common at both extremes of society but, according to Dublin, there were fewer suicides at the top of the pyramid than at the bottom. This final diagnosis was based upon a study of a series of files from Metlife's insurance investigators for three successive years: 1929, 1930 and 1931. In each of these three years, the suicide rate was much higher amongst holders of insurance policies designed for those on small incomes (industrial policy holders) than amongst clients who were better off in economic terms (ordinary policy holders). The findings obtained by Louis Dublin are particularly reliable. Quite apart from their quality, which is guaranteed by the international reputation the statistician enjoyed at the time, the origins of this source are very important: given the financial stakes, it is very much in an insurance company's interest to make a very careful distinction between suicides, homicides and accidents. Every case is very carefully investigated.

The study carried out a few years later (for the period between 1937 and 1956) by the American sociologist Elwin Powell (1958) provides our third source. It deals with a conurbation in Oklahoma. It provides by far the most precise information on the distribution of suicide among different social groups. The study was carried out in the town of Tulsa, a conurbation in Oklahoma with a population of some 250,000. The county of Tulsa is essentially urban; less than 3% of its population is regarded as 'rural'. The city, which is fairly typical of the Mid West, is almost evenly divided between white collar workers and blue collar workers. The rate of unemployment ('seeking work') was 11% at the beginning of the period. At the beginning of the 1940s, the war industry – aeronautics – and growth breathed new life into the economy. There were fewer unemployed, more births and more access to home-ownership: Tulsa was America's ninth city in terms of home-ownership.

The average income for an economically active man rose to $3,000. Oklahoma City, one hundred and fifty kilometres to the west and of comparable size, had a lower average income. More murders and fewer suicides took place there.

During the twenty-year period between 1937 and 1956, 426 of those aged 14 and over in Tulsa took their own lives, which gives an average rate of 13 per 100,000. At this time, Tulsa ranked thirty-ninth in the American cities' suicide league, and Oklahoma was eighty-ninth. The variations in the suicide rate were quite in keeping with the trends observed in the major developed countries, especially in Europe, during the same period. The suicide rate for white males was four times higher than that for women (27, as against 6) and ten times higher than that for blacks (2.7 per 100,000). The male suicide rate rose with age, whilst the female rate varied less with age (showing a small peak at between 35 and 44 years of age). Elwin Powell was particularly careful to establish data on the occupational status of those who took their own lives. He completed, case by case, the data collected by the Public Records Office for death certificates by systematically going through the two local papers that immediately reported the vast majority of the suicides that occurred during the period. When there was a discrepancy between the information published in the press and that given on the death certificate, Powell pursued his investigations by contacting families, neighbours, work colleagues, etc. He thus succeeded in establishing a detailed picture of the occupational status of 94% of the community's residents who committed suicide between 1937 and 1956.

During the Second World War, both male and female suicide rates reached the lowest point recorded since 1917. Having said that, the war did not bring about a proportional fall in the suicide rate in all social categories. The suicide rate amongst supervisors, managers, employees in the service sector and unskilled workers fell by 40%, whilst that for sales clerical and office workers, both skilled and unskilled, fell by only 20%. Throughout this twenty-year period, the highest rates again applied to the two ends of the professional hierarchy, whereas the rate for average groups remained constant and relatively low: 24.6 for 'professional managers and sales clerical', as opposed to 19.6 for industrial and other manual workers. The former suicides were more premeditated, and the latter more impulsive. The maximum age was the same: 48.2 for white collar workers and 45.2 for blue collar workers. Eighteen per cent of the blue collar suicides occurred outside the city, as opposed to only 2.8% of white collar suicides.

Turning to the managerial category, suicide rates were higher amongst salaried managers, civil servants and, right at the top of the table, self-employed proprietors, who had the highest rate of all.

Table 8.1   Suicide rates per 100,000 according to occupation

White collar		Blue collar	
Pharmacists	120	Taxi drivers	87
Doctors	83	Welders	25
Nurses	38	Bus drivers	17
Lawyers	36	Truck drivers	12
Engineers	15	Mechanics	10
Accountants	7	Carpenters	5

Pharmacists and doctors had a particularly high suicide rate, whilst engineers and accountants had low rates. No suicides were recorded amongst writers, publishers, journalists, clergymen, or primary and high school teachers. The suicide rate amongst nurses was six times higher than the average for women, whereas that for women sales clerks was below average. Among the blue collar workers, the suicide rate for taxi drivers was four times the male average, whereas that for truck drivers was below average. The highest rates were found amongst men who had no occupation: the retired (89 per 100,000).

In short, suicides in Tulsa between 1937 and 1956 occurred, as Olive Anderson and Louis Dublin observed in previous periods and different geographical contexts, at the two extremes of the social scale, and there appear to have been slightly more at the top of the scale than at the bottom. As elsewhere, certain professions in Tulsa had very high suicide rates: doctors and nurses, lawyers and taxi drivers. In the nineteenth century, coachmen had a reputation for committing suicide more often than other groups.

Our fourth and final source is another American study. This study was carried out in a Chicago conurbation after the Second World War (Maris 1969). It reveals a significant reversal of the trend observed up until then. The study was very detailed: 2,153 certificates recording deaths by suicide were examined for the period 1959–63 in Cook County, which includes the city of Chicago. It gives the sex, age, race, matrimonial status and occupation of every victim. Data from the Public Records Office were compared with and supplemented by those from the coroners. Chicago's suicide rate (8.8 per 100,000) was very close to the average American rate. It was 11.5 for whites and 3.6 for 'non-whites', most of whom were black. The trend had definitely been downwards from 1925 onwards (it reached 15.3 in 1925). In the Chicago of the early 1960s, as in all European countries at that time,

Table 8.2   Chicago 1960. Suicide rates (per 100,000)

Upper social status	15
Middle social status	13
Sales workers, craftsmen	20
Workers	46.4
Labourers	51

there were more suicides in the spring than in winter or summer, and on Mondays rather than other days of the week. Men, old people, the single and the widowed committed suicide more often than women, young people and the married. From the beginning of the century onwards, there were fewer and fewer suicides in the towns, and more and more in the countryside.

Ronald W. Maris's study was the first to observe a definite reversal in the distribution of suicide across social groups. The structure was no longer bimodal. Chicago's suicide rate rose the lower down the social hierarchy Maris went.

According to this study, suicide rates were very high amongst police officers, hairdressers, housewives, nurses and farmers.

The distribution of suicide in Chicago anticipates that which came to prevail in France and most of the developed countries in the second half of the twentieth century. Suicide no longer haunts the more affluent section of society, and is now concentrated amongst the poorest and the most fragile. The authors of an English study (Drever and Bunting 1996) have calculated the suicide risk associated with various socio-professional groups. Using the official nomenclature that divides the working population of Britain into five categories, they observe that suicide rates are much higher in the fifth category than in the first two. At the very bottom of the social hierarchy, class V includes semi-routine and routine occupations, whilst classes I and II include managerial and professional occupations, intermediate occupations. It is no longer the affluent classes that have the highest suicide rate; on the contrary, it is the social categories situated at the very bottom of the social scale.

As societies became more affluent in the twentieth century, the richest and most highly educated categories, which were once as much at risk as the poorest, appear to have found ways of reducing the risk of suicide and of protecting themselves against it. How are we to explain the fact that suicide's social centre of gravity has been displaced downwards?

First clue: many more social bonds

We can begin to try to answer this question by using, for the moment, a strictly Durkheimian explanatory logic, whilst extending its field of application. Let us look at the quality and intensity of the social bonds that give individuals reasons to live by giving them the feeling that they belong to a whole that is greater than they are. According to this hypothesis, the upper classes should nowadays enjoy the benefits of greater social integration. Durkheim essentially reduced these bonds to the domains of the family and religion. We can now extend them to include the bonds created by professional life, associations and, more generally, all contemporary life's forms of sociability.

There are many data that confirm this hypothesis, notably the 'Contacts' survey carried out by François Héran in the 1980s (Héran 1988a, 1988b). This study of patterns of sociability in France, which was carried out on behalf of INSEE, compiled a detailed record of how many encounters, conversations and meetings with other people an individual had in the course of a week. This explored the concrete forms taken by the main forms of sociability: kinship, friendship, neighbours, contacts at work and with the service sector, and included encounters with shopkeepers, the health service, teachers and even strangers. The findings were clear: sociability is greatest amongst the intellectual sections of the upper classes. Teachers, artists, managerial staff in the civil service have as many contacts as members of the liberal professions, even though the latter are wealthier, whilst administrative and retail managers are a long way behind them, with engineers in an intermediate position. Primary school teachers, nurses, social workers and middle managers in the public sector have more contacts than craftsmen, shopkeepers, technicians and foremen. Workers, for their part, differ from other groups in that they have a lower level of sociability: fewer friends, fewer mates, fewer contacts at work and less contact with shopkeepers or neighbours. Kinship is the only area of sociability in which they are on an almost equal footing with other groups.

These findings upset received ideas about sociability in the population. Whereas the upper intellectual categories represent only 10% of the active male population, they accounted for 34% of all recorded relations of friendship, 35% of all work contacts, 24% of contacts with family and 23% of contacts with neighbours. The reverse is true of workers. Although they were the largest group (35% of working men) at the time the survey was carried out – 1982–83 – workers accounted for only 17% of contacts with friends, 15% of contacts at work and 15% of contacts with neighbours. As the various components of sociability tend to be cumulative rather than exclusive, working-class categories, as opposed to intellectual ones, tend to suffer from a lack of social contacts, which is one of the contemporary indicators of what Emile Durkheim called integration. The social hierarchy of sociability, as measured by this survey, in fact reaffirms the social hierarchy of suicide.

The same is true of membership of associations. The survey shows that the higher an individual's position in the social hierarchy and the more qualifications the individual has, the greater the chance of joining an association – teachers and social workers are ahead of all other social categories in this domain. Most associations – cultural or sporting associations, civic associations and groups set up to defend collective interests – now provide the individuals who join them or who are active in them the same psychological and moral support that the Church or involvement in parish activities once provided. Programmed meetings and encounters with other people, the feeling of being useful and recognized, and of existing as such in the eyes of others, a relative social mix, parties, the enjoyment that comes from involvement in unpaid collective activities with goals that go beyond individual interests, and from the use of energy and skills acquired at school or at work. To take only one example: the increase in the number of choirs in France over the last thirty years, which recruit the vast majority of their members from the middle and upper classes, shows that the economic and social preconditions for access to this warm and gratifying form of sociability are costly in terms of both time (one or two rehearsals per week) and resources (familiarity with musical notation, personal effort . . .). It is therefore not surprising to find that associations recruit most of their members from the most highly educated strata of the population.

At the same time, the transformations undergone by villages and working-class neighbourhoods have led to the disappearance of a whole host of family or neighbourhood-based associative practices that once allowed all families to be involved in activities based upon mutual aid at little cost to the individuals involved. Either the village population moves away or, if the village is close to an urban centre, those who work in the city move to the countryside in large numbers. Henri Mendras (1962) calls this process 'rurbanization'. In the working-class neighbourhoods, pockets with the best locations become gentrified, whilst the estates become marginalized. Whilst the number of choirs has risen, the number of town bands has fallen drastically. With respect to church attendance, it is more common amongst the upper categories than amongst the working classes.

To remain in the same register, an INSEE survey on lack of well-being published in 2003 also shows that relational isolation is much more common at the bottom of the social hierarchy (Pan Ké Shon 2003). Being on a low income, having no qualifications, living on an estate or stating that 'it's hard to get by' are closely associated with relational isolation. It is mainly groups living on modest incomes that are affected by isolation. On top of that, they experience loneliness and boredom; although they are more rarely on their own, young people are more likely than most to be affected by these feelings of boredom and loneliness. The greatest sensitivity to lack of well-being is to be observed amongst those whose situation is to some extent precarious: the unemployed and disabled people who are unable to work. 36.8 per cent of these people state that they find it difficult to make ends meet and 28.2% of those living on estates also say they suffer from a lack of well-being.

In a word, the general hypothesis about the benefits of integration formulated by Durkheim one hundred years ago still holds today. We have only to extend the field of the social bonds that tie individuals to the collectivities that surround them, and to all the areas of sociability, and to make a distinction between social milieus, to find that the richest and most highly qualified groups are better integrated than the others and are therefore better protected against the risk of suicide.

The major interest of INSEE's survey of relational isolation and lack of well-being is that it shows that the situation of people suffering in this way is not reducible to a lack of contacts or relations with others. It takes the form of a feeling of loneliness and boredom and, more generally, a lack of well-being. Is this a type of mental suffering? Yes, but it is not only that. As we have seen, suicide mainly affects populations whose life expectancy is short. Because he stresses only the individual's relations with the group, Durkheim locates the social causes of suicide at the level of individual interaction for those who commit suicide because of a lack of integration, and in the domain of individual psychology in the case of anomic suicide: individuals lose sight of the markers that once allowed them to adapt their behaviours to fit in with the rules prevailing within their social groups and to adjust their desires to their possible satisfaction. The founding father of sociology therefore greatly underestimated the existence of an organic substratum that is largely a product of economic and social constraints, and which can destroy those bonds and disorient individuals. He does of course include economic crises, price changes, bankruptcies, etc., but he remains at a very general level and he never takes individuals' material living and working conditions into account. When he does finally discuss mental illness, it is in order to assert that there is no link between suicide and madness, suicide and neurasthenia, or suicide and alcoholism. The data accumulated over the last century by epidemiologists, doctors, psychiatrists, ergonomists and occupational sociologists in all countries refute this hypothesis. There is indeed a link between suicide and mental illness, and between suicide and alcoholism. But these states and symptoms are never necessary and sufficient causes of suicide, as they only appear in very specific economic and social contexts.

Second clue: making the best of it

All these new data suggest that we have to include a new link in the causal chain that connects 'the social' to individual suicides. This link comprises the effect of material living and working conditions on individuals' state of mental and physical health, or in other words, on their actual bodies. This does not mean reverting to a biological causality by making the state of the living organism the cause of suicide. On the contrary, we remain within the framework of the sociological explanation outlined by Durkheim and simply extend the spectrum of social variables that are taken into account to include the very different pathologies that affect individuals, depending on the position they occupy within society and at work. It is now impossible to regard the body as a natural reality that is governed by the laws of biology alone. Our bodies are now moulded and shaped by social life, which even determines how long they last. It is in this context that Halbwachs was already discussing death as a social phenomenon and taking the view that the point at which it happens results largely from working conditions and hygiene, from the attention that is paid to tiredness and illnesses and, in a word, to conditions that are as social as they are physiological. As the philosopher and doctor Georges Canguilhem puts it (1966: 161):

> In short, the techniques of collective hygiene which tend to prolong human life, or the habits of negligence which result in shortening it, depending on the value attached to life in a given society, are in the end a value judgement expressed in the abstract number which is the average life span.

The 'clerical and manual workers' category stands out from all other because it has a shorter life-span and a very high mortality rate from all causes of death with the exception of AIDS. The greatest disparities between the group of senior managers and that of the liberal professions relate to causes of death associated with alcohol (the rate of deaths from cirrhosis and tumours in the upper respiratory and digestive tracks is 10 times higher), diabetes, respiratory diseases (rate of deaths is 5 times higher), vascular cerebral accidents, cancer of the stomach (3 to 4 times higher), accidents at work and road accidents, myocardial infarctions, cancers of the intestine and pancreas (2 to 3 times higher) and . . . suicide. Whatever the cause of death, mortality rates fell much less steeply for the clerical and manual workers group in the periods 1979 to 1985 and 1987 to 1993 (Jougla *et al.* 2000). The greater vulnerability of this group was obviously related to its poor living and working conditions.

One domain that is of especial relevance for our purposes is that of the social distribution of cardiovascular pathologies and the way it has changed during the last fifty years. The way it has changed has much in common with suicide, and may provide keys that can explain why the most educated and affluent social categories were, in the second half of the twentieth century, less at risk of suicide, and why the risk of suicide became, like heart disease, concentrated amongst the least well-educated and poorest categories, which were more vulnerable to poor living and working conditions.

Deaths from cardiovascular disease are now most common amongst working-class categories (Lang and Ribet 2000). This has not always been the case. At the beginning of the twentieth century, more affluent circles were the worst affected. The reversal occurred in the period 1940–1960, at the same time and under the same conditions as the reversal of the trends for suicide. Once again, the decline in the mortality rate was not the same in all milieus. It fell by only 14% amongst manual and clerical workers, whilst it fell sharply amongst managerial staff (−47%). The incidence and lethality of these pathologies were at their greatest amongst workers. They were more at risk and, when they did fall ill, were more likely to die than other groups. Managers, on the other hand, were less likely to fall ill and less likely to die when they did so. Clerical workers occupied an intermediate position within this domain. Although they often fell ill, they were less likely to die. It is difficult not to establish a link between their greater exposure to cardiovascular pathologies and their living and working conditions (Bosma, Peter, Siegrist and Marmot 1998). Many studies of stress at work have been undertaken during the last twenty years. The conditions that lead to stress have now been clearly identified: excessive or insufficient work loads, too little time to finish the job, no recognition of reward for work that is well done, uncooperative superiors, colleagues or subordinates, job insecurity, no control over or pride in the finished product, serious consequence or a minor mistake of a brief lapse in concentration, and so on. All these negative and anxiogenic factors are effects of the three great forces that have transformed the world of work so profoundly over the last twenty-five years: the intensification of work, growing job insecurity, and the introduction of flexible working patterns (Baudelot, Gollac *et al.* 2003).

The American occupational psychologist Robert Karasek and Johannes Siegrist, a German professor of medical sociology, have elaborated two complementary models to explain heart disease, and have tested them against the health statistics (Bosma *et al.* 1998). According to Karasek, a high level of psychological demand coupled with a low level of decision-making capacity lead to stress, which can be heightened by social isolation at work. For individuals exposed to these constraints at work, the relative risk of coronary disease or death from it varies between 1.3 and 4. It is therefore a major risk factor. The second model, that developed by Siegrist, assumes that it is the disequilibrium between the efforts workers are prepared to make and the rewards they expect (monetary recompense, professional recognition, etc.) that defines the stress situation. Working conditions are not the only factors involved, unemployment also has a part to play. A longitudinal study carried out in Great Britain shows that the risk of death from cardiovascular disease in the five years following the appearance of symptoms is twice as high amongst subjects who have experienced periods of unemployment than amongst those who remain in continuous employment.

The obvious explanation for the discrepancy between the incidence of cardiovascular disease and its lethality lies in social disparities in the available recourse to healthcare. In most Western countries, members of the least advantaged groups are in a poorer state of health, they seek medical care less often and receive a lower level of care (Lombrail 2000). Surveys carried out in France by CREDES and INSEE[3] show

---

[3] Centre de recherche, d'étude et de documentation en économie de la santé (Centre for Research, Study and Documentation in Health Economics: CREDES) and Institut national de la statistique et des études économiques (National Institute for Statistics and Economic Studies: INSEE).

that disparities between social groups are more pronounced in terms of preventive care than in healthcare as a whole (between 18% below 27% above the mean of an index standardized in terms of age and gender). The working classes seek help later than other groups. There are also great social divisions when it comes to seeking psychological and psychiatric help.

The combination of working and living conditions leading to anxiety and stress and delays in seeking help of poorer quality hastens the premature deaths of the many manual and clerical workers suffering from cardiovascular disease. This gives us a better understanding of how the best-educated and richest social categories – who are much less exposed to insecure and stressful working and living conditions, who are well aware of the risks involved and who enjoy access to higher quality care – have been able gradually to protect themselves against this risk by improving their diet, adopting a healthier lifestyle and seeing a doctor regularly. The same explanation applies to suicide. Being less exposed to insecurity, to the threat of redundancy and, more generally, to the harshness of life, those occupations that are at the top of the social scale and who live in the big cities enjoy better living conditions and social networks, and better health facilities. They are better at consulting doctors before they lapse into depression and despair. They enjoy much more secure and comfortable living conditions, and that gives them better control over both the future and their day-to-day lives. Modern societies have succeeded in providing their elites with the inexhaustible resources that allow them to improve their quality of life and life expectancy continuously. In their view, nothing is more precious than life: their professions make their jobs interesting, their income gives them access to an infinite and varied range of consumer goods, and their qualifications mean that many sources of cultural interests are available to them. For other people who are less affluent, death can seem preferable to living in hell.

Modern forms of poverty

This is all the more so in that poverty is no longer what it used to be. Serge Paugam, a sociologist at the Centre Maurice-Halbwachs, explains (2005: 88–93) why suicide in rich countries affects the poor by making a distinction between *disqualifying* poverty and *marginalized* poverty, and above all *integrated* poverty. 'Integrated poverty' is precisely the social reality to which Durkheim was referring when he stated that 'poverty protects'. Many poor people come within this category, but there is little difference between them and other sections of the population. They do not constitute a group in their own right, and their condition is the same as that of their region or country. They are not particularly stigmatized. Their standard of living is low, but it is made tolerable by the intensity of the relationships they have with their family, neighbourhood, village or region. Solidarity is a collective and individual response to adversity. People stick together and individuals are not isolated. This type of relationship with poverty is found during the 'economically backward' stage characteristic of traditional or pre-industrial countries. As we have already seen, such countries typically have the lowest suicide rates.

The form of poverty most commonly found in rich and developed societies is very different. Serge Paugam describes it as 'disqualifying' because it devalues and stigmatizes the individuals concerned by gradually excluding them from all forms of involvement in economic and social life. Because they are excluded from work or have very precarious jobs, they are handicapped in several ways: they are on low incomes, live in poor housing, are in a poor state of health, and their family and support networks are fragile. Being dependent on social transfers and welfare, they feel that they are, in social terms, quite useless. 'I am trying to find a job for a man who has reached the end of his life', states a 61-year old artist. 'We are the people no one needs any more,' states a steelworker who was laid off for economic reasons at the age of 48 (cited in Fassin 2000). The loss of social value leads to a loss of self-respect. Following Robert Castel (1995), Serge Paugam shows how this new form of poverty spread in all the developed countries from the early 1970s onwards thanks to both the rise in unemployment, increased job insecurity and underemployment (part-time work). The curve in the suicide rate, and especially amongst young people, began to rise in both France and other countries at precisely the same moment. The intensification of work and the spread of continuous production flows increased stress levels considerably and led to anxiety. Poverty no longer looks like a steady state, as it did in the context of integrated poverty; it rather looks like a demotion and a loss of status. Becoming poor in a rich society or falling into the poverty trap leads to much greater suffering than being poor in a poor society. For someone living in a society in which the social identity and status of individuals is largely based upon their involvement in productive activity and their position in the job market, and on their ability to convert the rewards they receive for their labour into consumer goods, exclusion from the main source of social and economic values can be experienced as a tragedy. The new forms of poverty generated by rich societies further weaken those they affect in every area of life: health, housing, income and contact with others. Hence their great vulnerability to a whole set of risks, including suicide.

Suicide is revealing: it exposes deep divides between the top and bottom of the social scale in terms of health, life expectancy and well-being. Suicide forces us to take these deep divides into consideration. We are a long way away from the explanations proposed by Durkheim, which are essentially based upon social integration. All the data gathered by psychiatrists and epidemiologists tends to relate suicide to depressive states and alcoholism. The richest members of our modern societies seem to have discovered ways of avoiding these situations, or of finding a cure for them by turning to the most sophisticated forms of medicine. The poor, who are more at risk, still seem to be excluded. This 'materialist' explanation does not, however, contradict the 'social' explanation. We simply have to rethink the terms of the argument. Durkheim's explanation is much too organicist. Individuals are not integrated or marginalized as a part of some macro-organism. Their integration into society is based upon their total involvement; what is at stake is the meaning of life and even the status of the subject (the *self*, as defined by the American sociologist George Herbert Mead (1934). Someone who finds a place as a subject in the social game is integrated, and his or her existence is recognized by others. Being integrated and becoming integrated means playing the game ('*illusio*' as Pierre Bourdieu, who could be a Latinist when it suited him, put it). It means joining in a social game in which what we ultimately expect is not just some recompense for our contribution, but the validation of our status as subjects. Many studies have shown that job insecurity and unemployment lead to fewer contacts with other people. When you drop out of the game, sociability loses its meaning. We also know that some of the unemployed improvise new roles for themselves and become involved in new and significant interactions in order to go on living within a social game. The youngest sign up for vocational courses and become or go back to being students. The eldest describe themselves as retired. Such tragicomedies reveal how important work is when it comes to constructing a personal identity.

Modern industrial society, which has often been described as anonymous and individualistic, does not seem to encourage people to join in the game. Organizations define status and roles without reference to individuals; companies are interested in potential and performance. Having neighbours does not necessarily mean that we know each other in modern towns. However, this place of anonymity and negation of the individual is far from being homogeneous. As Halbwachs noted, as we go further up the social hierarchy of work, the individual's interpretation of his or her function becomes more important than the mere implementation of routine procedures. A manager working at the interface between many anonymous organizations can use his function to enrich his network of connections considerably. Those who are in this privileged position establish whole networks that extend far beyond the solid core of familial sociability. These networks may well be *weak*, but they are also extensive and effective. At the other end of the chain for those who are led to think that 'anyone could do *my* job', minimal involvement in work compensates for the lack of interest in the routine tasks they carry out: they are reduced to making self-fulfilment coincide with family life. The civilizing of manners allows those who can play a much more involved role to make use of anonymous spaces where their personal identity is protected from intrusions (buses, bars, restaurants, waiting rooms . . .).

The ethnologist and psychiatrist Georges Devereux (1951) saw some features of our culture – the distance between people, the abstract nature of relationships, the absence of any specific spatial configuration – as providing one of the bases for a dominant clinical picture: that of schizophrenia. In contrast, once initiated, a Plains Indian can easily explore the whole of his culture and have personalized relationships with all the people around him who define his precise role in its social institutions. Modern society acts at a distance: no one deals directly with all the people their actions mobilize. We need specialists to tell us precisely what the effects of our initiatives will be, even when it is a matter of passing on a material or cultural heritage. As a result, our identification with our roles is no more than partial and we do not fully involve ourselves in relationships with others. We are involved in a sort of vast 'human comedy', in which an incomplete socialization paves the way for a splitting of the ego or, in extreme cases, schizophrenia. But this situation can have many advantages for those who have a wide range of resources. When we suffer adversity, mobilizing only those people with whom we have always had close relationships can prove to be a source of comfort, but it is not very effective; inside the solid core of the family, we all have much the same resources. On the other hand, calling on a vague acquaintance because we know he or she is competent in one particular area may prove indispensable when we are looking for a good lawyer or a medical specialist.

The American sociologist Mark Granovetter (1973) has demonstrated the strength of *weak* networks when it comes to looking for a job or a house. For managers, a sociability that has been acquired in the workplace is certainly a trump card, even if it is based upon partial or superficial emotional commitments. We might add that valuable and opaque demarcations between jobs or between company capital and private property can make us immune to even shocking reversals of fortune. The image of the banker who commits suicide after going bankrupt has had its day. *Potius mori quam foedari* – death before dishonour. A number of recent scandals (Crédit Lyonnais, Dae Wo, Meissier and Vivendi Universal, France Télécom, Guillaume Sarkozy and Les Tissages de Picardie) are there to remind us how far we have come since the days of Sombart's *Le Bourgeois* and Balzac's *César Birotteau*. The disjunction between roles (officials versus administrators, shareholders versus sleeping partners . . .) means that we can now construct personal identities that are sheltered from risks and needs. And anonymity is not without its charms when it allows us to cultivate secret gardens and to have accounts in tax havens . . . without losing the benefits of fame. The complexity of social involvement can, for those who are in a position to take advantage of it, provide solid defences against the risks that are always present in a culture based on 'creative destruction'. Those who find themselves at the very bottom of the social ladder do not have the same resources at their disposal.

Health, both mental and physical, is one of those commodities whose accessibility is dependent upon our cultural capital. Those in managerial positions have long been preoccupied with their physical image. They keep an eye on their weight, go on diets, take physical exercise to compensate and have regular check-ups. They look after their bodies as though they were a form of capital. Their bodies are in fact part of a relational life in which they have to if not be attractive then at the very least –partial investment requires it – seem to be attractive. For a long time, workers and peasants used medicine as a way of belatedly repairing a machine that had broken down. Reliance on preventive and sophisticated medical techniques, the early diagnosis of depressive states and the possibility of receiving healthcare without alerting and alarming those around us are real possibilities in rich countries. Provided that we are in a position to use them on a day-to-day basis.

Towards a cultural and social minimum wage

Modern societies erect high barriers between the rich and the poor. This is not simply a matter of how material goods are distributed. In the richest societies, wealth tends to become less concentrated. It is only during periods of depression that inequalities reappear. At such times, inequalities are no more than a measure of the uneven accumulation of material goods. Only those who are in possession of social and cultural capital can really make effective use of modern wealth: keeping fit, the optimized use of cutting-edge medicine, reliance on psychological support, an informed attitude towards consumerism, being happy at work, an enlightened use of the law and relatively easy access to a wide range of formative cultural goods.

Even when they do own material goods (according to INSEE, 51.5% of skilled workers and 31.4% of unskilled workers owned their primary residence in 2004), the working classes, in contrast, do not enjoy all the satisfactions of modern life. Their only defence against the most repetitive jobs, which are meaningful only in terms of the material goods (assets) they provide, against their housing conditions (far away from the city centres), against their children's difficulties at school and against the threat of redundancy and unemployment is . . . their family.

Amartya Sen, the winner of the Nobel Prize for economics, has always insisted (1992) that societies should provide all their citizens with a minimal 'capacity' to exploit available wealth. He refers to this as 'capability'. In his view, the lack of capabilities, or in other words individuals' inability to choose what looks good to them, is a better measure of poverty than the inability to satisfy what are seen as basic needs. He concludes that what must be fairly distributed as a matter of priority is not income, but the capacity to develop 'human functionings' in order to allow everyone to lead a dignified and meaningful life. He therefore invites economists to take into account not only material goods but also freedom of speech, dignity, self-respect and involvement in social life in general, or in other words, all the things that turn an individual into an integrated social being who is recognized as such by others. His observations about very poor countries also apply to our modern societies. The invisible division of wealth between economic capital, cultural capital and social capital leads to great discrepancies in terms of basic securities. The solutions to the ordinary or extraordinary difficulties of social life available to a person with a degree who speaks a foreign language are not available to workers and peasants who face competition from all over the world but who are forced to remain within their own national boundaries.

9 And yet Women Survive . . .

One of the most commonly occurring ratios to have been revealed by suicide rates over the last two hundred years, and one that is quite ignored by classical sociologists, is the differential ratio of men to women. In 1995, in the 78 countries whose suicide rates were known, the respective averages were 18.7 per 100,000 for men and 5.8 for women. On average, the male suicide rate is therefore 3.2 times higher. Using the more restricted statistical basis of 6 countries during two periods of time, Durkheim concluded (1897: 50): 'On average, for every woman who kills herself, there are an average 4 male suicides. So each sex has a determined predisposition to suicide, which is constant even for different social milieus.' The greater statistical accuracy for 1995 notwithstanding, we therefore have the same balance sheet for the nineteenth century and the late twentieth century. Should we seek the reasons for this stability in innate male and female constants? In the sexual stereotyping that leads boys to take an interest in weapons of destruction, and girls in childcare? In the persistence of the warrior virtue of courage and the symmetrical virtue of a narcissistic respect for one's own body? The ways in which people commit suicide – hanging and firearms in the case of men, and poison and drowning in that of women – would suggest that we do.

But is the consistency as great as Durkheim claimed it to be? Figure 9.1 (page 162), which records the ratio between female and male suicide rates in 78 countries in 1995, is very informative. The factors that lead to variations in the suicide rate from country to country have the same overall effect on men and women. The coefficient of correlation is exceptionally high (0.86). The protection enjoyed by women is constant only in terms of averages. We are not talking about a constant in physics. Several other points should also be noted. There is only one exception to the rule that the suicide rate is higher amongst men, but it is a major exception: China. In contrast, the high suicide

Figure 9.1 Male and female world suicide rates, 1995

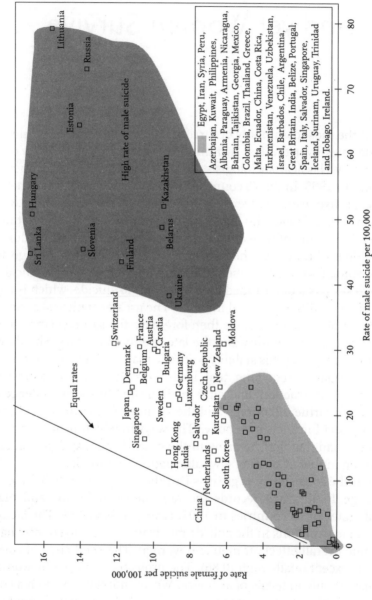

Source: World Health Organization, *Figures and Facts about Suicide*, 1999.

rates in the former Soviet bloc go hand in hand with an exceptionally high rate amongst men (Ukraine, Estonia, Lithuania, Russia and Belarus). In southern and south-eastern Asia, in India, South Korea and Singapore, the female suicide rate is very similar to that for men, and brings us closer to the extreme case of China.

In similar social situations, three to four times fewer women than men commit suicide. These 'social situations' are, of course, stripped to their bare essentials: age, marital status, region and country. Similarities in these details tell us nothing about the respective amount of time that men and women devote to family life and managing family relations, and it tells us even less about their respective involvement in various aspects of social life. That does not matter. The ratio of 1:4 was verified in the nineteenth century and confirmed at the end of the twentieth. It is verified by all the available series for most countries, and appears to be a natural constant. And that is how Durkheim saw it. He says nothing, or almost nothing, about this huge difference because he regards it as a natural fact, and therefore as something that is of no interest to sociologists. After a century of progress in education for girls and a few decades of gender studies, some of Durkheim's texts on the differences between men and women seem to belong to a different intellectual world. As we embark upon the twenty-first century, the fact that men are at greater risk – or that women are less at risk – has to be regarded as a social fact in its own right. It is, however, a social phenomenon of a very special kind because it almost never varies.

The children come first . . .

The explanation for the persistence of this difference has to be sought in the transcontinental and transhistorical invariants in the gender-related construction of personal identities. Durkheim's primary finding, which lies at the heart of his basic intuition, can provide us with a starting point. Having noted that married individuals of both sexes enjoy the same degree of protection, Durkheim concludes at the end of a convincing statistical analysis that it is not marriage as such that is the deciding factor, but the presence of children.

Now childcare is one of the clearest distinguishing features of the gender-related construction of personal identities in all societies. No change in methods of production has eradicated the fact on which all methods of production are based. The male realm consists of distant places, trials of strength with nature and the handling of weapons;

the female realm, of domestic spaces centred upon the 'production' of men, large and small. Amongst the Gouros of the Ivory Coast, hunting elephants, accumulating metals and managing granaries are exclusively male activities and are associated with the political privileges of primogeniture. The women are responsible for cooking and bringing up children. The same contrast can be seen in the 'time budgets' of contemporary France. Despite the tumultuous social changes of all kinds that have occurred, time budgets have changed by only a few minutes over the past fifty years. Women still do most of the housework (almost two-thirds in terms of the overall time spent on it during the week), and the time men devote to housework daily increased by only eleven minutes between 1986 and 1999 (data from INSEE's 1999 *Emploi du temps* survey, cited in Bihr and Pfefferkorn 2002). In Germany, 'modernist' couples claim to share the housework, but 'egalitarian' husbands divide their time into two big blocks: the time they spend at work and their contribution to housework, which is concentrated into one or two days. Women do not experience this clear-cut dualism: they spend the whole week navigating, to use Christine Garbe's metaphor (Garbe 1993), their way through an archipelago in which the islands consist of their children's activities inside and outside school, shopping and various administrative chores, and finally, their professional occupations. These contrasts in roles and status inform the primary socialization of both boys and girls. The games girls are encouraged to play revolve around human relationships. Boys are steered towards outdoor games, the domination of nature and demonstrations of strength. No world could be more influenced by the naturalism of gender than the world of toys. Sales assistants invariably ask customers about the age and gender of the child they are buying for and thus equate the two (Vincent 2001).

Whereas boys are encouraged to compete with their fellows, girls are trained from childhood onwards to become involved in the generational cycle. This applies not only to their children but also to their entire circle of relatives. Even today, women are responsible for keeping up relations not only with their own families, but also with those of their partners. It is women who sustain the family's collective memory: forenames, birthdays, various events.

Irrespective of their marital status, women are integrated into a solid core of intergenerational relationships. Their sociability is more restricted in terms of volume, but it is also more structured than that of men. Because they are detached from many of their families' concerns, men construct extended networks of weaker ties. Their networks are richer but more fragile, effective in terms of mobilizing resources and gaining power, but strongly characterized by competetiveness. For the moment, we will restrict the argument to this contemporary extension of Durkheim's theory.

The Chinese exception

Exceptions to the seemingly natural constancy of the male/female ratio can, however, tell us something about the respective reasons why women and men commit suicide. We will look first at the exceptionally high suicide rate amongst women in southern and south-eastern Asia, which has been studied on a country by country basis by the many researchers who have tried to pinpoint its origins in the particularly tense nature of conjugal relations there. We will begin with China with what really does have to be called the 'Chinese exception'. China is the only country in the world where more women than men commit suicide.

Danielle Elisseeff (2001), a great specialist on Chinese civilization, relates the phenomenon to the prevailing concept of suicide and to the nature of the conjugal relations within which a married women must define herself and to which she must submit. In a virilocal society, a young wife is subjected to very strong pressures, in particular the pressure to produce a male heir, and to the strong social control brought to bear by the family into which she marries. If she fails to live up to expectations, she has a lot to lose: she may lose her dowry and reputation, risk repudiation and have to accept de jure or de facto polygamy. In extreme cases, her life is at risk. In this Asian context, many observers suggest (Elisseeff 2001, 57–58) that the *revenge suicide* model should be used to describe female suicides in particular:

In the Far East, suicide is not considered to be dreadful or shameful. It is a way of bearing witness. When a senior civil servant who is honest commits suicide, his death tarnishes the government. When a married woman commits suicide, she brings shame on her mother-in-law, and her father is entitled to ask the courts for compensation. Reaching that point certainly presupposes a lot of suffering, but there is no personalist religion to forbid suicide in China. Chinese peasants will never have any difficulty in finding cellars containing a rope with which to hang themselves, or a fishpond or wash-house where the water is deep enough for them to drown themselves. But whilst some are driven to suicide by poverty,

Chinese women also commit theatrical forms of suicide, or conspicuous and accusatory forms of suicide that point the finger at brutal husbands or mothers-in-law. Their image can never be restored. Women also know that suicide allows them to take a vengeance that is slow, refined and cruel: for the rest of their lives, their torturers will be persecuted by the dead woman's ghost night after night, so that their every member will tremble and they will always dread the coming of twilight. [. . .] The slightest accident and the smallest anomaly will be attributed to the woman who committed suicide and her tormentor will, with a bit of luck, eventually die of terror.

Danielle Elisseeff's analysis is corroborated by the sinologist Léon Vandermeersch (2002), who sees in it an opportunity to further qualify Durkheim's analyses, which pay too little attention to the power of dogmatic representations:

Many works provide abundant proof of this, the most famous being *Tales of Vengeful Souls* by Yan Zhitui (AD 531–590). This is an anthology of the most edifying examples of how ghosts represent the invisible hand of justice. That is enough to encourage victims of injustices of all kinds to commit suicide so as to find their place in the supernatural world, where they can exercise the power of retribution that is attributed to spirits. This calls into question Durkheim's thesis that, in terms of their influence on suicide, 'Detail of rituals and dogma is secondary. The essential is that these rituals and dogmas should be of a kind that nourishes a sufficiently intense collective life' (Durkheim 1897: 178). The problem is that Durkheim's work on suicide looks only at the Catholic, Protestant and Jewish confessions. A study of Chinese society would have shown him that the rituals and dogmas of an animistic religion, which is an even greater force for integration, can mask some very strong suicidal tendencies.

The recent data show that it is mainly young women who have a very high suicide rate, especially in the countryside. Between 1987 and 1995, male and female suicide rates in the towns converged, but the gap remained constant in the countryside (see Figs. 9.2, 9.3, 9.4 and 9.5 (pages 167–70)).

In their very detailed case studies of contemporary China, the sociologists Sing Lee and Arthur Kleiman (2000) note the high incidence of suicide as resistance amongst women in the Chinese countryside. This can take the form of refusing a forced marriage, taking revenge against a brutal husband or despotic in-laws, or rejecting birth control when a woman has been unlucky enough to have a daughter for her first child.

Figure 9.2   China: evolution of male and female suicide rates in towns

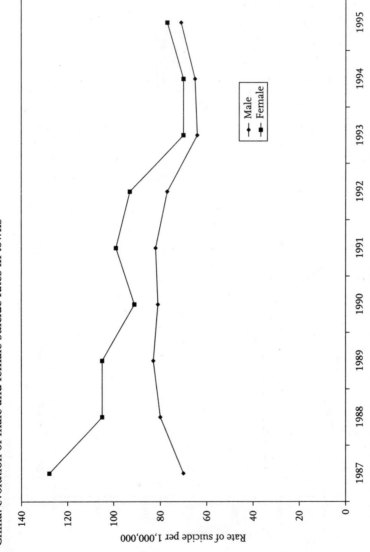

Source: World Health Organization, 1999.

Figure 9.3 China: evolution of male and female suicide rates in the countryside

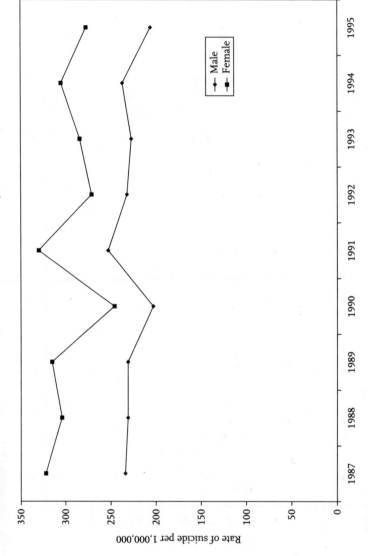

Source: World Health Organization, 1999.

Figure 9.4 China: male and female suicide rates in towns, by age

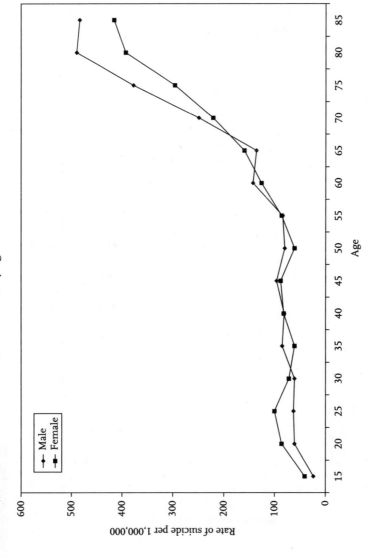

Source: World Health Organization, 1999.

Figure 9.5 China: evolution of male and female suicides rates in the countryside, by age

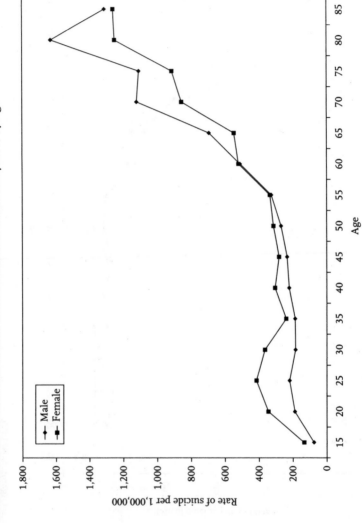

Source: World Health Organization, 1999.

Asia and the Pacific: marital problems

A more attenuated version of the Chinese model, which is without parallel anywhere else in the world, is found in other Asian countries where the suicide rate for women is not higher than that for men but has for a long time come close to it, especially in India. Abbé Dubois noted the phenomenon as early as 1816 in a work published in London (Dubois 1985: 273):

> Although murder and suicide are viewed with greater horror by Indians than by any other people, murders and suicides do sometimes occur amongst them. Murder is usually committed with poison. As for suicide, it is almost always women who are guilty. Driven to despair by the cruelty of a brutal husband, by the harassment of a shrewish mother-in-law, or by all the domestic dissensions to which Indian households are so often prone, they commit a criminal act against themselves in order to rid themselves of a life that has become unbearable.

Dubois was a missionary who was quick to pass judgement, but he was also an ethnographer who was familiar with portrayals of Indians, and he never confuses the sacrifice of widows on the funeral pyres of their husbands (*suttee*) with the suicides he is describing here. Although he disapproved of both, he knew that *suttees* were the object, 'in the Indian spirit', of 'an unbreakable attachment to these practices', which mainly affected higher classes and castes, whereas suicide was both condemned and widespread in all milieus (1985: 317).[1]

In 2000, Indian suicide rates were as follows:

In India, as in China, female suicide rates are at their highest at the ages corresponding to the status of young wives. At the ages of between 15 and 29, the suicide rate for women is higher than that for men. After the age of 45, the status of women changes and female suicide rates fall and diverge widely from the male rate. The importance of marital problems is confirmed if we take into consideration the presumed causes of suicide recorded by the Indian police authorities. The picture that emerges leads us to very different conclusions for men and women.

According to the Indian police, the association between female suicides and events within families is much closer. But this is especially true during the critical period of the first decades of married life (15 to

---

[1] The whole of Part II, Chapter XIX is devoted to the analysis of *suttee*. Dubois transcribes the word as *sâti*.

Table 9.1   Male and female suicide rates by age (India, 2000)

	Men	Women
15–29	13.9	14.6
30–44	22.2	13.9
45–59	24.9	10.6
60 and over	16.3	6.4
All	12.8	8.8

Table 9.2   India 2000: presumed causes of suicide by age and gender

		Family problems	Economic problems	Illness	Other	
15–29	Men	28.5	14.9	18.4	38.2	100
	Women	42.8	7.8	14.7	30.4	100
30–44	Men	25.7	12.7	21.9	39.8	100
	Women	36.5	6.8	20.7	36.0	100
45–59	Men	22.2	16.2	28.7	36.2	100
	Women	24.7	7.6	29.5	38.3	100
60 and over	Men	15.3	9.1	39.6	35.9	100
	Women	14.3	5.3	40.8	39.5	100

Source: National Crime Research Bureau (NCRB), table 28, pp. 119–120.

44 years of age). We can therefore conclude that the high female suicide rate for that age group is attributable to the difficulties of married life in a male-oriented world in which in-laws make formidable demands, especially for male children, and have the power to ensure that they are met.

Riaz Hassan's brilliant study (1983) of suicide has similar comments to make about Singapore. In 1970, women's coefficient of preservation in couples of Indian or Chinese origin began to rise only when they were 35. As many women below that age commit suicide as men, and about twice as many women aged between 15 and 24 as men do so.

The autochthonous Malays, who are Muslim, have very low suicide rates. This is particularly true of women. The low level of protection enjoyed by Indian and Chinese women under the age of 50 is therefore related to the nature of conjugal relations in the societies from which they come.

It is possible to confirm the importance of marital problems by taking into account the causes of suicide presumed by the coroner. In Singapore, the sociologist Riaz Hassan paints a picture of the causes

Table 9.3 Causes of suicide, Singapore, 1970

Age	−24	25–39	40–54	55–69	70+
Men	mental illness	mental illness	physical illness	physical illness	physical illness
	failure	physical illness	poverty	loneliness	loneliness
	physical illness	failure	loneliness	poverty	poverty
	unsatisfying work	poverty	mental illness	mental illness	mental illness
Women	mental illness	mental illness	physical illness	physical illness	physical illness
	physical illness	physical illness	poverty	loneliness	loneliness
	family problems	failure	mental illness	poverty	poverty
	unhappy in love	family problems	loneliness	mental illness	family problems

of suicide supplied by the coroner, according to age and gender, as follows.

Male suicides are associated with illness and life's setbacks (especially dissatisfaction at work and above all poverty). For women under 40, family problems are still the main cause. Riaz Hassan's study dates from 1970. But recent statistics confirm that women enjoy little protection: between 1970 and 1995, the protection enjoyed by women remained, on average, almost unchanged, and rose from 1.5 to only 1.6 (WHO), whereas it was equal to or greater than 3 in all Western countries.

Revenge suicide in New Guinea

The theme of revenge suicide is also central to Dorothy Ayers Counts' research (1984) on the Lusi women of New Guinea. Suicide in protest against ill-treatment on the part of husbands and in-laws is one of a number of culturally defined forms of resistance at the disposal of women (appeals to male relatives, personal responses, appeals for the help of other women, passivity), but it is the last resort. As a rule, the women make sure that their suicides and the reasons behind them are known to everyone. Suicide is often a public act: the vengeful intentions are clearly stated and the individuals against which they are directed are explicitly named. The women achieve their goals: the reactions of the men and women of the villages recorded by the ethnologist often support women who commit suicide, who thus exercise a form of power or counter-power.

The link between the violence of male domination and female suicide is very clearly revealed by an account of two societies in New Guinea: the Baruya and the Ankave (Bonnemère 1992).[2] Male domination is clearly established in both societies, but it takes different forms. In the case of the Baruya, the disjunction between the sexes during adolescence is heavily emphasized during the initiation; there is no recognition of maternal lines of descent, and sanctions are often violent. Women often resort to suicide. In 9 out of 10 cases, the immediate cause is a quarrel between husband and wife. Suicide is usually accompanied by obvious signs of vindictive intent:

> The groups involved [in the suicide of a woman] may be reluctant to renew matrimonial alliances that have ended so badly (the Baruya practise a restricted form of exchange). On a day-to-day basis, if we can put it that way, a woman's suicide deprives her husband of someone who is indispensable to him because she is the one who tends the garden, feeds him and gives birth to and brings up his children. But a man's suicide can also be the result of an act of female resistance. A Baruya may take his own life because his wife refuses to cook for him, is reluctant to perform domestic tasks or, worse still, has insulted him in public.

Amongst the Ankave, who have greater recognition of descent through the maternal line, both male and female suicide is unknown.

> No collective lessons are organized to teach girls to be submissive towards men. The preconditions for strong male solidarity do not exist, and boys do not have a totally negative image of the world of women. As a result, the dissymmetry between the sexes is less pronounced and relations between couples are more egalitarian. The division of labour, in particular, is relatively flexible. It is, for example, possible to see women climbing to the top of a tree to gather arec nuts, or men holding babies in their arms. The forms female resistance takes amongst the Ankave seem to be in keeping with the lower intensity of antagonism between the sexes.

[2] Although it is fashionable for so-called 'qualitative' sociology to insist that the observation of a limited number of cases should be described as 'ethnographic', Bonnemère's article is based upon an analysis of 1,500 deaths amongst the Baruya and 400 amongst the Ankave. The Baruya files were compiled by Maurice Godelier.

Japan falls into line

Japan presented a similar picture in the 1960s: women enjoyed little protection (1.6 on average), but their degree of protection increased as they grew older (1.5 at the age of 25, 1.6 at 35 and 1.9 at 55 and over). From the 1970s onwards, women, and especially young women, began to enjoy greater protection; at the same time the trend for male suicides was to remain stable whilst there was a clear decline in the female rate. Japanese economic growth appears to have been accompanied by a gradual resolution of the difficulties traditionally associated with marriage.

The data on the links between suicide and marriage derived from studies of Asian societies would not, however, have appeared odd to any careful reader of Durkheim. By analysing the links between suicide and divorce, Durkheim made three important discoveries. On the one hand, the suicide rate falls as the divorce rate rises, though that finding could quite easily have been deduced from the General Register's statistics and from the protection afforded by marriage. Durkheim's statistical ingenuity then allowed him to make a much more important discovery: the fact that there is a link between the higher number of suicides and the rising divorce rate does not simply result from a rising suicide rate amongst divorced people. Divorce leads to higher suicide rates amongst the married. Durkheim also discovered that the rising divorce rate affects married men and married women in completely different ways: husbands enjoy less protection, and wives enjoy more protection.

If we look again at conjugal relations, and in particular at the most brutal forms of male domination, our analysis of suicide has to take account of an anthropological dimension that escapes Durkheim and even Freud: the revenge orientation. Perhaps it is a factor that influences suicide in industrialized societies. Think, in particular, of the young suicides who encounter not only anomie but also unfairness (better qualified, less well treated) in the job market or who have difficulty in developing a personal identity.

Why don't more Western women commit suicide?

One problem affecting the richest Western countries remains. As we know, there have been major changes in the situation of women over the last fifty years in such important areas as the acquisition of qualifications and access to jobs. Traditionalists raise the spectre of a unisex society! Although we still have a long way to go before we reach that stage, even in the Scandinavian countries, the fact remains that the status of men and women has in many respects converged. We might therefore expect to see a convergence of male and female suicide rates. But we find nothing of the kind: between 1970 and 1995, the gap widened in the United States, Canada, Australia, New Zealand, Spain, Italy, Norway, Austria, Hungary, Japan, Great Britain and Germany. There was no change in Sweden, Switzerland or France. Ireland was the only country in which the gap narrowed from an exceptionally high level of protection (6.0) to a level close to the world average (3.9).

But the most extraordinary phenomenon of all concerns young people. Although the rising suicide rate amongst young people has for fifty years been a salient feature in all countries, the gap between male and female suicide rates for those aged between 14 and 25 has increased almost everywhere, except in Belgium and the Netherlands, where it remained wide and stable throughout this period. The gap between men and women grew wider in Argentina, Australia, Austria, Brazil, Canada, Chile, the Czech Republic, Finland, France, Greece, Israel, Luxembourg, Mexico, New Zealand, Paraguay, Poland, Singapore, Slovenia, Spain, Sweden, Switzerland, Uruguay and Venezuela (WHO 1999).

We can corroborate these findings by taking a more synthetic view and noting that there is no correlation between the two indices for women's involvement in economic and social life, which has been calculated by World Bank researchers on an annual basis since 1995, and the gap between male and female suicide rates. [3] Even when women's rate of involvement comes closer to men's, there is no change in the difference between their respective suicide rates. If we replace that indicator with the sex-specific indicator of human development, which includes differences in income, levels of education and life

[3] The *indicator for women's involvement* in economic and social life was calculated for each country, and includes three components: the share of GDP attributable to women's work on the basis of the ratio between female and male wages, and women's rate of activity; the percentage of active women employed in technical or managerial positions or in the liberal professions; the proportion of women elected or appointed to parliament. The *sex-specific indicator of human development* also has three components: women's share of waged income, women's life expectancy and women's level of education. Since 1995, both indicators have been calculated annually by the United Nations Development Programme. For more details on how they are calculated and on their international distribution, see UNDP [PNUD] 1995.

expectancy, we find a slight but insignificant increase in the gap. Recent changes in the position of women in the richest countries have therefore had no impact on suicide rates by sex. Indeed, amongst young people, whose suicide rate is rising all over the world, the gap shows a tendency to increase because men are much more affected by the phenomenon.

The work of the Canadian economist John F. Helliwell (University of Vancouver), which looks at 117 international studies, sheds some light on these findings: the social and cultural factors that either encourage suicide (the rising divorce rate) or discourage it (sociability, trust in institutions, religious belief) affect men and women in the same way, but the strength of their impact differs: with the exception of a belief in God, which does more to protect women than men, the other variables, most of which relate to socio-economic organization, have a much greater impact on male suicide rates (Helliwell 2004).

We have already noted more than once that female suicide rates are less sensitive than male rates to variations in the economic situation, unemployment and inactivity, as well as to differences in social conditions and even age: the variations in the female rate are always less pronounced in those categories that are most and least suicide prone than those in the rate for men. Despite improvements in women's education, and despite women's clearly expressed desire to establish themselves in the job market, women appear to be less affected by social crises. Without wishing to provide a definitive explanation for this – the data are insufficient – we can make several suggestions: crisis or no crisis, women are always more exposed than men to an unfavourable job market; they always find it more difficult to get their qualifications recognized; when it comes to planning their academic and professional careers, they always tend to have parameters other than strict profitability on the job market. Adversity and their readiness to accept multiple responsibilities therefore inure them to the world's harshness. 'Situational poverty protects', as Durkheim might have said if he had read Bourdieu.

Even when he is involved in family life – present or future – a young man has first and foremost been trained to play the traditional role of the 'breadwinner'; the primary purpose of his studies is to prepare him for a prestigious professional position. When an employment crisis occurs, it poses a threat to his original hopes and destroys the meaning of his social investments . . . his whole masculine identity is called into question. Now the increase in the suicide rate amongst young men over the last thirty years is primarily bound up with the crisis affecting job prospects. Male and female attitudes towards work, and the way men and women view it, are strongly influenced by the traditional division between the sexes and the way it is internalized. Although men and women are becoming more equal, they still continue to view work in different ways.

Women's involvement in their work is very different to that of men, whose work revolves around power, money and the desire to leave a lasting legacy. Women are much more sensitive to the day-to-day aspects of their professional activity, and experience them in more personal ways; they are much more interested in the immediate content of their work ('I throw myself into my work because I'm interested in it') and the attention they receive as individuals ('I feel that people listen to me and I like that'). Human contact and the pleasure of helping others seem to relate to a much more female concept of work. When it comes to describing a 'good job', men emphasize the wages issue, whereas women talk about the hours they work. It is clear that these different value judgements are largely the product of an objective and structural inequality that is bound up with women's involvement in work in the domestic sphere (Baudelot, Gollac *et al.* 2003).

Even though they are involved in economic competition and the uncertainties of professional life, women are still responsible for housework and its management. They have not aligned their behaviour with that of men. Whilst all these inequalities protect women from suicide, they reveal, in their own way, basic differences between the respective status of men and women. Although still incomplete, the silent revolution of the twentieth century does hold out the promise of a different division of values and contributions.

Conclusion: A Lesson in General Sociology

The impact of society on suicide is perhaps the greatest enigma to have confronted sociologists ever since Durkheim. Why do more men than women kill themselves? Why more old people than young? Why do more people living in the countryside than in the cities kill themselves? Why more Protestants than Catholics? Why are there fewer suicides on Sundays than on Mondays? Why are there more in summer than in winter? Why are there fewer suicides in wartime than in peacetime? Developments in sociology and ethnology mean that we have reliable data for all these questions on a global scale.

Our two-hundred-year-long world tour teaches us a powerful lesson in general sociology. The vast majority of suicides follow both short- and long-term social trends. If society can leave its mark on one of the most personal of acts, it impacts even more clearly on the other aspects of life.

Suicide rates always rise during economic crises, and fall during wars. Suicide is in phase with economic development during the nineteenth century, but it goes against trends in economic development in the twentieth. It therefore shows us that war is not just 'a continuation of politics by other means', and that an economic crisis is not just a 'structural adjustment'. They are the affects of each and every one of us who are thrown into turmoil by these cataclysmic events. The objective future that society offers people of all classes cannot be thrown into turmoil without consequences. It provides the basis for the most personal predictions and projects.

Although it pays attention to broad trends, our study also gives 'exceptions' the importance they merit. China is the only country in the world where more women than men commit suicide. India, China and Russia are the only countries to have experienced a rise in suicide rates in the twentieth century comparable to that experienced under nineteenth-century capitalism. In the case of Russia, it has been much worse.

A statistical analysis of suicide rates allows us to correct many stereotypes.

If there is one society that has been stigmatized because of its obsession with qualifications and its male domination, it is surely Japan. And yet, if we exclude the most recent period, we find that, in the second half of the twentieth century, the Japanese suicide rate falls in all age groups and that the gap in male and female suicides increases considerably. This is doubtless because Japan has succeeded in inventing new forms of integrative sociability, whilst at the same time modernizing its economy and relations within the family. Whatever the explanation may be, the situation in France is much more worrying.

We also find, on the other hand, that what appear to be the most spectacular transformations have little impact on social structures inherited from the past. Much has been made of Mao's sensational declaration that women 'hold up half of heaven'. No doubt they do hold up half of heaven when it comes to goals, but not when it comes to equality between boys and girls at birth. As in the past, suicide is still one of the weapons of protest that Chinese women can use in their struggle against the traditional contempt in which their sex is held and against ill-treatment by their in-laws. Although its political orientation is very different, India has not succeeded in ridding itself of this scourge, as we can see from both its exceptionally high female suicide rates and the proportional deficit in the number of girls born.

The construction of socialism in Russia had the same effects on suicide as the construction of capitalism in the European countries of the nineteenth century. The suicide rate rose steeply in both cases. William Pitt and Joseph Stalin, the Corn Laws[1] and the five-year plans all had the same effect. Forced marches in the direction of industrialization take no heed of a society's political orientation.

The sociology of suicide also reveals the profound impact of developments that can look like minor reforms to someone who does not pay them the proper attention. Until the first half of the twentieth century, suicide rates in European countries peaked in the month of August and seasonal differences were very marked. The introduction of paid holidays changed that pattern: the months of July and August

---

[1] Cobden abolished England's Corn Laws, which were a protectionist measure to restrict the import of grain, in 1846.

became the low points in the seasonal curve of the suicide rate, and seasonal differences also became less pronounced as urbanization progressed. The spectacular fall in the summertime suicide rate reveals how important it is to bring families together and to include a little bit of the 'leisure civilization' in the cultural and social minimum wage enjoyed by all social classes. Our social lives are no longer governed by the rhythms of agricultural activity, but by those of the educational system, with its holidays and new terms. The ministerial decision to give children a day off school on Wednesday rather than Thursday from 1972 onwards had a considerable impact on the female suicide rate. Until 1972, there was a regular fall in the suicide rate for both men and women: it was at its highest on Monday and at its lowest on Sunday. Since 1972, fewer women have committed suicide on Wednesdays than on Mondays, Tuesdays, Thursdays or Fridays (Aveline, Baudelot, Beveraggi and Lahlou 1984). Durkheim was right after all: looking after children does protect against suicide.

If, in short, we attempted to trace the effects of social and economic change affecting society as a whole on our day-to-day lives, sociologists would never be short of work. That is how Durkheim understood it, and all the colleagues who have accompanied us on our journey never fail to refer to him.

Sociology doesn't explain everything

It goes without saying that economic and social conditions, and cultural and religious values, influence variations in the suicide rate. But it would be a mistake to end this account of our travels simply by saying in more scientific terms: 'what is truth on one side of the Pyrenees, is error on the other.' In all the countries we have been looking at, men and women basically interpret suicide in the same way: it is a serious and aberrant act, and the probable explanation for it lies in depression, madness, unbearable illness, and the extreme difficulties of living in society. People are the same from Palawan to Brittany, from St Petersburg to the Malay archipelago: the act of suicide concerns us in the same way and causes us the same confusion. No matter where or when the act is committed, it involves serious contradictions between the demands of social life and the fate of individuals.

That is the conclusion Jean La Fontaine reaches in her study of forms of suicide amongst Uganda's Gisu tribe (La Fontaine 1967). In this self-sufficient agrarian society, bad harvests affect the male suicide rate because the men are responsible for the production and distribution of foodstuffs. They have no effect on the female rate. Most cases of female suicide result from conjugal violence, especially when women try, unsuccessfully, to return to their lineage of origin. Suicide amongst men peaks during the years following their circumcision: when they become adults, they find it hard to tolerate the fact that power and the distribution of wealth are monopolized by their elders. Those who try to find a way out by emigrating to European-owned farms in order to build up some savings of their own experience even more tensions when they go back home to claim what is rightfully theirs. Suicide amongst young adult males is almost always associated with the difficulties young men have in finding their own niche in kinship networks. As Paul Bohannan (1967) emphasizes in his conclusion, traditional African societies are sound enough to find a peaceful solution to the problems created by married life and the coexistence of different generations. Even though their suicide rates are much lower than those of our societies, suicides do, however, result from unresolved frictions in these domains, which are central to their social life.

Things are not very different in our developed countries. A study published in 2002 shows that young homosexuals are very much at risk from suicide. It confirms the findings from the United States, Canada and Australia. The authors comment on the great loss of self-esteem amongst young homosexuals who are confronted with the demeaning stigmatization of homosexuality within the family or at school; this has a disastrous effect on their personal development.[2]

In the nineteenth century, the French police saw reversals of fortune, jealousy, illness or disappointment in love as the main causes of suicide; the Indian police listed very similar reasons in 2000. The inhabitants of Palawan, who associate good mental health with hard work, sociability and good humour, use a very rich and subtle vocabulary to describe suicides and paint a picture very similar to that of depression: grief, abandonment, loneliness, isolation, anxiety and fears for the future (MacDonald 2003: 434–435). The anthropologist's comments also shed light on the social conditions in which suicide occurs in Singapore; however, once these have been explained, the European reader has an intuitive understanding of the meaning of the messages left by Malaysia's Chinese and Indians at the moment of

---

[2] This epidemiological study (Shelly 2002) was carried out by the AREMEDIA Association in collaboration with INSERM.

their deaths. In a statistical study of the determinants of suicide in China, the authors (Phillips, Li and Zhang 2002) demonstrate that, when they have been adjusted by sex, age and place of residence, eight significant factors for predicting suicide can be identified: a high level of symptoms of depression, previous suicide attempts, acute stress at the time of the suicide, a poor quality of life, a high level of chronic stress, interpersonal conflicts in the preceding two days, a member of the family who has previously presented with suicidal behaviour, a friend or colleague presenting with suicidal behaviour. The probability of suicide increases greatly as the number of risk factors rises. In short, and despite the substantial differences between the characteristics of the populations that commit suicide in China and in the West, the risk factors are, at the individual level, very similar.

Sociology is thus faced with contradictory demands:

- Variations in the suicide rate demonstrate the extent to which the structure of societies influences the personal development of individuals, but suicidal crises are very similar in all countries. Suicide is the object of social disapproval in almost all societies. In the Western Catholic tradition, suicides were denied a religious burial. In the African populations studied by Paul Bohannan, the tree from which a man has hanged himself must be uprooted.
- Suicide risks vary from group to group, and are influenced by historical changes, even those of a material nature. The risk of suicide is therefore a legitimate object of sociological study, but the causes which, in any given society, lead an individual to commit suicide elude sociology because suicide remains an individual and exceptional act in all milieus and all social conditions.

We therefore must return to the links between psychology and sociology, as traced, albeit somewhat sketchily, by Durkheim. If one thing is certain, it is that individual psychology cannot explain the difference between suicide rates for Paris and the provinces, between the English and the French, or between Catholics and Protestants. As Durkheim rightly remarks (1895: 129): 'Every time a social phenomenon is explained by a psychological phenomenon, we may rest assured that the explanation is false.' But he takes the rejection of psychology much further than that. Any attempt to relate suicide to a psychological variable is, in his view, immediately suspect. He denies, for instance, that there is any link with mental illness or alcoholism. And yet contemporary Russia provides living proof of the parallels between the fluctuations in suicide rates and the consumption of alcohol. The drastic measures introduced by Gorbachev did considerably lower the suicide rate over a two-year period, but it remained much higher than in Western countries. The development of a scientific epidemiology mobilizing psychiatrists, help lines and medical centres has led to the conviction, based on detailed case studies, that suicide is usually related to depressive states. It is no longer possible to deny the importance of personal factors.

The reason why Durkheim is so suspicious of psychology is that he secretly hopes to be able to explain not only variations in suicide rates but suicide as a whole. That is how we have to interpret the construction of the curious chapter on individual forms of suicide, which are said to be 'determined' by anomy, altruism or egotism. Inspired by an unashamed imperialism, Durkheim writes (1897: 317):

> In reality, there are very different kinds of suicides and these differences are discernible in the way in which the suicide is carried out. So we can classify acts and agents under a certain number of heads and the types correspond, in their essential character, to the types of suicide that we previously outlined according to the social causes behind them. They are, as it were, the prolongation of these causes inside the individual.

Sociology should be able to explain, if not everything, at least the essentials. The Durkheim who is so scrupulous about his choice of data and criticisms of them constructs his ideal types of suicide with broad brushstrokes and borrows his information from the literature at random. Contemporary psychiatry has, thanks to psychological autopsies, the study of personal and family history, and neuropsychiatry, gathered a rich harvest of data about individual risk factors. It is therefore tempting to piece together the social statistics and the epidemiological findings. This is what Pierre Surault (2003: 64) tries to do when he outlines his explanatory schema (see Fig. 10.1, page 185).

The explanatory model is attractive. Its main value is heuristic, and it invites us to establish links between changes in affectivity and the most material aspects of life in society. We can in fact conclude that individuals' social conditions predispose them, on an unequal basis, to experience stress, loneliness, depression and addictions; their recourse to affective prevention is equally uneven. Such are the implications of François Héran's work on sociability, Serge Paugam's work on the effects of modern poverty, and Dominique Schnapper's work on the ordeal of unemployment (1991). For a sociologist, research into the causes of suicide is a powerful stimulus. Surault's model has yet to integrate the findings of our present knowledge.

Figure Conc. 1   Interaction between variables

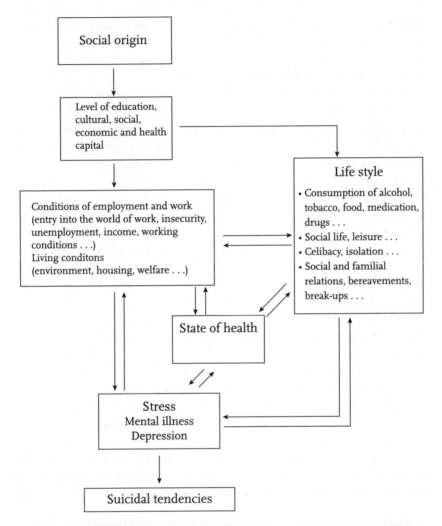

Source: Pierre Surault, 'Approche socio-démographique de la santé mentale', *Actes de la journée de restitution régionale ARPCIMEP–ORSPEC*, Poitiers, 1 October 2003, p. 64.

There is a discrepancy of scale between the increasingly sophisticated statistics used by sociologists and the observations of psychiatrists. According to WHO, one million people commit suicide
every year all over the world, almost 11,000 of them in France. The
sociologist's observation post looks out over a period of several years
and a growing number of countries. In contrast, when psychiatrists
collate their data, they base their arguments on at best a few hundred

observations. The sophistication of the data is inversely proportional to its scale: psychiatrists can use psychological autopsies, life histories, medical files and accounts of personal or family history. Sociologists are reduced to working with a stereotypical skeleton of variables such as sex, age, occupation, marital status and place of residence. They therefore reach very different conclusions.

Summarizing the findings of his studies, the epidemiologist Jean-Pierre Kahn identifies three types of risk factor: primary risk factors (psychiatric problems, previous suicides and suicide attempts on the part of the victim or his or her family, talking to others about suicidal intentions, impulsiveness leading to actual suicide); secondary risk factors (whose predictive value is poor in the absence of primary factors, or what he calls 'seriously negative life events', such as the early loss of parents, social isolation, separation, divorce or death of a partner, unemployment or serious financial factors) and tertiary risk factors that have no predictive value in the absence of primary and secondary factors; these include masculinity, age (and especially adolescence and senescence), certain vulnerable periods, such as the premenstrual phase in women and the summer period for everyone.[3] Thus, for the medical epidemiologist the principal social 'causes' of suicide (economic situation, age, gender . . .) appear to be factors of a secondary or even tertiary nature, devoid of any predictive value. There is nothing surprising about this: in an acute situation, which is where they make their diagnosis and, when they can, take preventive measures, psychiatrists deal primarily with personal factors. Suicide is always an exception even amongst those populations that are most at risk of it, and it can never be ruled out, even amongst those populations that are least at risk. Individual psychology and history make all the difference. That it is difficult to reconcile the sociologist's telescopic view and the psychologist's microscopic view

[3] 'Psychological autopsy is a method developed in the United States in the 1960s. Its primary purpose was to clarify the causes of death in which suicide was suspected but not clearly proven. It is based on an *a posteriori* investigation of interviews with the suicide's family, the analysis of medical sources, gathering information about family or individual history, and the psychology and lifestyle of the deceased, his or her relationships, and events in the period leading up to death. These data are compared with the objective data relating to suicide bids in order to determine whether or not suicide did occur. Psychological autopsy has rapidly become an interesting method for documenting the existence of psychiatric or somatic problems and the nature of the care the individuals concerned had enjoyed' (Jean-Pierre Kahn, lecture delivered at the Collège national des universitaires en psychiatrie, CHU Angers, 2005).

should not be a cause for surprise. A change of scale results in different perceptions.

The dispute between the historian Robert Dion and the geographer Daniel Faucher over the planting of vines in France provides a good example. According to the historian, vines and especially great vineyards are found near big cities and the main routes of communication by sea and by river, and later by rail. A 1/100,000 scale map of France is a perfect illustration of this principle of localization, which is further confirmed by historical research. If, on the other hand, we study the terrain on a geographical basis and with topographical maps on a scale of 1/80,000 we find that, within any given region, vineyards are always located on the most favourable or least unfavourable *terroirs:* well-drained, stony slopes that are south-facing and protected from the mists that rise from the ground water in the valleys (Côtes de Moselle, Coteaux de Jurançon). 'Ecological determinism is therefore just as obvious as urban and commercial determinism' (Bertrand 1975: 49–50).

The historian and the geographer are both right about vineyards, just as the sociologist and the psychiatrist are both right about suicide. Their respective bodies of knowledge complement one another, but they cannot really communicate because their arguments are based on different scales. This is why the work of sociologists and demographers always creates such interest amongst epidemiologists, psychiatrists and psychologists, and Durkheim figures prominently in their bibliographies. But when the latter deal with individual cases, they rely on their own knowledge. Which is so much the better for their patients.

Is there a sociology of exceptions?

Suicide does, however, raise a particular problem for sociologists. When they use statistical methods to look for the social causes or meanings of suicide, they work by comparing rates. However, there is such a disparity between the numerator (the number of suicides) and the denominator (the population in question) that one cannot but wonder if this sociological undertaking is anything more than guesswork, as statistics are being used to quantify an exception.

Suicide and the level of education share a common characteristic: only statistics can clarify their social dimensions: for suicide from the late nineteenth century, through the studies of Durkheim and his predecessors; for social inequalities in schools in the early 1960s, through

INED's first studies. The same method is adopted in both cases. Individuals – school students or suicides – are grouped into broad categories (sex, age, occupation of parents or of the individual concerned, place of residence, etc.) and discrepancies in performance at school or in voluntary death between the different modalities of these categories are measured. The findings of the statistical analysis are expressed in the same terms: men commit suicide three times more often than women, and a working-class child is twenty-three times less likely than other children to gain admission to a *grande école*, there are more suicides in the countryside than in the big cities, girls do better at school than boys, and so on.

The two realities – suicide and education – are, in strictly statistical terms, quite different. From the late nineteenth century onwards, primary schools admitted all children, and the school population represented the population as a whole. In the twentieth century, schools, which have often been likened to businesses, were much bigger than the biggest firms. With their regular and mass comings and goings, schools naturally lend themselves to demographic interpretation: the concepts of educational aims and student mortality rates have been successfully compiled by demographers, and it is they who made the first quantitative studies of the years children spent in education (Girard, Bastide, Clerc and Sauvy 1970). The annual pattern of admissions and school-leavers suggested the metaphor of economic book-keeping as promulgated by Leontief. The phenomena quantified by the statistics – success or failure, the choice of future path, access to employment – are also realities that are experienced by school students.

Suicide, in contrast, only becomes a sociological object thanks to the sociologist's pen and calculator, and as a result of some very dubious mathematical operations. Individual cases, which are all very different, are added up and the relationship between the total number and the main social magnitudes is calculated. The population is broken down according to the categories of the General Register. The sociologist's object, the social suicide rate, that he calculates in this way, does not correspond to any lived reality. It is an artefact, pure and simple. In contrast, the rate of success or failure attained at any given stage of the school system measured by social category, gender or age group is similar to a school grading system, a reality familiar to any school student.

By studying actual trajectories and those supplied by longitudinal studies, the educational sociologist can adopt many different viewpoints, carry out surveys and gradually identify real trends. Every suicide, in contrast, is a point whose trajectory the sociologist cannot know. If we relate an individual suicide to the findings of demography by comparing rates, we draw an imaginary line between points that are far removed from one another: an individual tragedy, on the one hand, and masses that are summarily described in terms of place of residence, occupation, gender, age and marital status on the other.

That is not all. If our analysis traces the progress of a cohort of school students year by year and uncovers the social factors that lead to success or failure in reaching a given level, we can be confident that those individuals who experience the most disadvantages (in terms of gender, social and national origin, parents' cultural capital, residential area, number of years in pre-school education) will stand much more chance of failing than succeeding. The son of an unskilled worker, neither of whose parents is a graduate, has only a 21% chance of finishing secondary school, or in other words, of entering the fifth form [seconde] four years after entering the first form [sixième] (calculations based on Vallet and Caille 1996: table VI 2: 109). Conversely, those individuals who enjoy every advantage are almost guaranteed to succeed. The daughter of a manager, whose parents both have their baccalauréat, has an 88% chance of getting into the fifth form four years after entering the first form. The differences between these two categories of individuals are enormous: 67 points out of 100. The power of social determinants is obvious.

We cannot, of course, exclude individual factors. Some children who have every advantage do fail, and some disadvantaged children do succeed. Studying paradoxical trajectories is very instructive, provided that we recognize them for what they are. They sometimes provide an opportunity to further refine our social analysis and to discover pertinent microsociological trajectories beneath the macrosocial differences: differences at the level of social and cultural capital, the contradictory ways in which some restructured families pass on their capital, the compensatory effects of a particular school or teacher, subtle differentiations in the use of the written word in working-class milieus, and so on. There does no doubt come a moment when the sociologist has to give up the struggle. Failure neuroses, exceptional motivation and personal potential are not really sociology's concerns. Psychology, which has in-depth knowledge of schoolchildren's social and cultural environment, then intervenes at the end of the explanatory chain.

Suicide, in contrast, is an exceptional phenomenon in all societies and for both sexes, in all milieus and in every age group. The forces, impulses and crises that provoke suicide or that are associated with it are primarily individual. In contrast with what happens in schools, the vast majority of populations marked by all the social factors associated with suicide do not commit suicide. The vast majority of Breton widowers or bachelors over the age of 60 living in rural communities in Morbihan do not hang themselves. And suicides do happen in those populations that are marked by every protective factor. Lise Delamare, who was the model for Madame Bovary, was a married woman, a Catholic with two children and lived in a small provincial town. Despite all these protective factors, she still took her own life.

When it comes to suicide, gender and age have been the most determinant sociological factors since the nineteenth century. It is here that the differences are most marked. In France today, the probabilities that a man over 75 and a woman of 20 will commit suicide are very unequal: 151 chances in 100,000 in the case of the man, and 2.6 chances in the case of the woman. We must not, however, fail to take into account that the probability of not committing suicide is 998.5 chances in 1,000 in the case of a man over 70, and 999.9 chances in the case of a girl of 20. The gap between the category most at risk and the most protected category is no more than 1.5 chances in 1,000. Suicide remains the exception. It is obvious that here, in contrast with what happens in the example of schooling, psychology intervenes at the beginning rather than at the end. Explanations for, and the understanding or interpretation of suicide, are primarily a matter of individual psychology. The epidemiology of suicide, which aims to list all the risk factors in order to alert the doctors who care for those who pose a suicide risk, takes into account (along with a great number of genetic, psychological and health determinants) one environmental variable: the loneliness and solitude to which the individual is exposed. But epidemiological models are not primarily sociological (Abbar 2000).

The economy, integration and self-esteem

A comparison of the statistics for the nineteenth and twentieth centuries suggests that we should reflect on modern societies' forms of sociability and their undoubted strength, but also on their fragility and cost. The tendency of the suicide rate to fall during the course of the last century and the fact that it remains high in all rich countries reveals two different trends. On the one hand, modern societies tend to destroy traditional certainties, to 'disenchant the world' and to leave individuals to their own devices; they encourage suicide. On the other, they free individuals from the daily struggle for survival and open up personalized horizons for everyone, and therefore reduce the suicide rate. This objective contradiction, which is inseparable from the general spread of affluence, suggests that we have to challenge two extreme attitudes:

- The catastrophic and pessimistic vision, which claims that the development of capitalism will result only in exacerbated forms of individualism that leave everyone alone to their individual fates. All foreseeable developments will be regressive, everything will go from bad to worse and sacrosanct standards will fall. Let us look reality in the face: suicide rates are lower than they were in the nineteenth century, and they are even lower if we take the ageing of the population into account. We do after all have to remember, and Richard Inglehart's studies confirm it, that whilst money does not make anyone happy, it goes a long way towards doing so.
- The irenic liberal vision according to which all evils are no more than inevitable adjustments made by an invisible hand, for the greater good of all.

More modestly, the contemporary sociology of suicide brings us face to face with certain good old contradictions that have always divided the social world. Old versus young: the oil crisis was handled better by those who became rich before it happened. Poor versus rich: if we wish to have a share in the profits, we have to pay an entry fee, not so much in terms of material wealth as in terms of social and cultural capital, in Bourdieu's sense of the term. Rich countries versus poor countries: poor countries are still protected from suicide by the poverty that forces them to live by the logic of survival and exploitation.

The world statistics on suicide also reveal the major effects of four forces already described by Durkheim, but which are now articulated differently: religion, the family, age and gender.

To begin with religion, which has by no means died out. Durkheim contrasted different confessions: Jews and Catholics commit suicide less often than Protestants. Religion still provides a high degree of protection against suicide; however, confessional differences are less important than the fact of religious observance or non-observance, and of belief or non-belief. Male suicide rates in Ireland and Poland, which are both Catholic, are higher than those in Holland, and more or less equal to those of Norway and Sweden, which are Protestant countries. Which leaves us with the enigma of Islam. This is a religion that combines a hidden God with disciplined religious practice and personal ethical obligations. To adopt Ronald Inglehart's terminology, Islam appears to be a religion that has room for a culture of the self and creative individualism, but also for traditional discipline in countries which are almost all dominated by the struggle for survival.

As for the effect of the family, our world tour confirms the view of all those who think that the hackneyed theme of the 'crisis in the family' is no more than a smokescreen. By outlining a model in which integration is central to the explanation, Durkheim gives us much food for thought. One of his proofs is that the family offers protection. Although they have to meet additional costs, individuals with family responsibilities commit suicide less often than those without them. The picture of the nineteenth century painted by Durkheim (1897: chapter III) is still convincing. It can be updated for contemporary France.

Now, as in the past and for all ages, the fact of being married still protects individuals from suicide. The differences between divorcees and the single may well be becoming less pronounced, but their suicide rates are still higher than those of both married men and married women. Widowhood has very different effects on the two sexes. It has a major aggravating effect on male suicide rates, but it has no more effect than divorce or celibacy on women aged 35 and over. British statistics provide very similar findings. We can extend this picture to include the world as a whole by taking into account the very close link that exists between suicide rates and levels of fertility in different countries.

If, however, we wish to bring out the full significance of Durkheim's intuition in order to extend it to the macroeconomic facts we have observed, we must further embellish what is still a somewhat mechanical concept. A society integrates when it provides everyone with the wherewithal to build self-esteem through their interactions with others. The American sociologists George H. Mead (1934) and Erwing Goffman (1967) have convinced us of that. The evolution of suicide rates in the nineteenth and twentieth centuries shows that industrial and urban society has gradually succeeded in providing new forms of social reasons to go on living, and to plan for the future, as well as forms of interaction that are just as gratifying and effective as those that were once provided in the immediate environment by families and village communities. The wealthiest individuals in the richest societies can now live and develop their identities at the level of the global village by varying their degree of involvement and enjoying the many benefits of an anonymous society. Economic development has stimulated new forms of sociability which, thanks to communications and travel – both real and virtual – allows interactions with all the planet's inhabitants. Access to these new forms of self-development is, however, very unevenly distributed. It implies a high level of education, membership of networks, and so on. Those who, because of their initial level of education and their occupational position, have received only a very poor endowment have only limited access to the benefits of modern urban culture. And rising unemployment means that they are very much at risk.

As we have noted, suicide rates decline as the economy grows. Even during periods of growth, modern societies are still prone to what Joseph Schumpeter (1942) called 'creative destruction', which constantly destabilizes the most vulnerable populations. During the *Trente Glorieuses*, which generated well-being, security and increased purchasing power, some sectors of the economy paid the price for growth: marginal agriculture and steel-making, to name only two. In what we now call a period of full employment, workers were always haunted by the fear of unemployment, as we can see from studies carried out at the time. Economic growth does reduce the suicide rate in general terms, but the permanent reorganization of the economy has the opposite effect. Which is why suicide rates remain very high, even during periods of growth.

Unemployment has an enormous influence on the new gap between the haves and the have-nots. Thanks to the accelerated growth of the *Trente Glorieuses*, a new concept of employment has emerged in the richest societies. Individual investment in school success must lead to recognized qualifications, which are themselves sanctioned by relatively stable employment. This is central to the formation of a personal identity and self-esteem. That is why unemployment is such an ordeal, and why there is such a close link between youth unemployment and suicide amongst the young.

Education plays a central role in the construction of modern identities and has completely changed relations between the generations. The main objective of families is now to ensure that their children are in a better economic and social position than they are. The rise of unemployment and job insecurity after the oil crisis made that goal even more important for all social classes. Job insecurity mainly affects the young, whereas the older generations still enjoy the privileged status and wealth they acquired in earlier periods. The most spectacular phenomenon revealed by a study of the statistics is the reversal of suicide rates for different generations. After an exponential rise, suicide rates by age began to flatten out from the 1970s onwards: the suicide rate amongst young people rose, but the rate for their elders fell. The increase in the suicide rate amongst the young reflects a crisis in the development of individual identities. Unemployment, deskilling and increased insecurity for young people are not just deficits in terms of resources; they are signs of the non-recognition of personal values. Suicide also shows that relationships between age groups are real social relationships. The fact that suicide rates rise with age might have seemed like a fact of nature, so long as old age brought its share of cares and limited prospects for the future. We can no longer accept that this is the case, now that we know that suicide rates have risen amongst the young and remained stable or fallen amongst the old following the oil crisis. The vital trump cards held by the young and the old depend on the economic history of their country. The move from the Welfare State to neo-liberalism tends to make the old rich and the young insecure. This represents an inversion of the social norms that underpinned educational values for more than one hundred years. This is probably the most serious finding revealed by our study.

We have also left one strategic question unresolved by advancing only a few hypotheses. The unequal suicide rates for men and women allow us to identify a number of societies, most of them in Southern and South-Eastern Asia, where conjugal violence is especially brutal. This suggests that we should also be looking at the construction of the self, which is bound up with the ways modern societies define masculinity and femininity. Why, given that men and women increasingly enjoy a similar status in the richest societies, are male and female suicide rates still so different? Men and women do not appear to construct their personal identities on the same basis, even though they live in the same society. Which suggests that we need to study further the construction of gender in contemporary societies.

A statistical analysis of world suicide rates over two hundred years, using various fields of observation from the local *départements* to the whole world, and combining individual and regional data, suggests that we have to look at the links between our countries' economic development and their cultural development. Using this index in relation to a phenomenon that is exceptional in terms of both its statistical weight and its seriousness allows us to pinpoint the crisis factors inherent in world society; it also allows us to understand why our fellow citizens have reasons to go on living and hoping. Sociology can probably contribute little to epidemiology when it comes to determining the risk factors, but it can still contribute something. Its main contribution, however, is to suggest that suicide implies that we have to look at society in a different way.

References

Abbar, M. (2000) *Approche pharmacologique des conduites suicidaires*. Nîmes: Service de psychiatrie du CHU.

American Association of Suicidology (2004) *Surviving Suicide*. www. suicidology.org, summer.

Anderson, O. (1987) *Suicide in Victorian and Edwardian England*. Oxford: Clarendon Press.

Anguis, M., Cases, C. and Surault, P. (2002) 'L'Évolution des suicides sur longue période: le rôle des effets d'âge, de date et de génération', *Études et résultats* no. 185. Drees, August.

Atkinson, T., Glaude, M., Olier, L. and Piketty, T. (2001) *Inégalités économiques (Rapport du Conseil d'analyses économiques)*. Paris: La Documentation française.

Avdeev, A. and Monnier, A. (1996) *Mouvement de la population de la Russie 1959–1994: Tableaux démographiques. Données statistiques* no. 1. Paris: INED.

Aveline, F., Baudelot, C., Beveraggi, M. and Lahlou, S. (1984) 'La saisonnalité du suicide', *Économie et statistique* no. 168, August.

Baudelot, C. and Establet. R. (1999) *Durkheim et le suicide*, 5th revised edn, collection *Philosophies*. Paris: PUF.

——, Gollac, M., Bessière, C., Coutant, I., Godechot, O., Serre, D. and Viguier, F. (2003) *Faut-il travailler pour être heureux?* Paris: Fayard.

—— and Establet, R. (2005) 'Classes en tous genres' in M. Maruani, ed., *Femmes, genre et société*. Paris: La Découverte.

Beaud, S. and Pialoux, M. (1999) *Retour sur la condition ouvrière*. Paris: Fayard.

Bertrand, G. (1975), *Histoire de la France rurale*, vol. 1. Paris: Seuil.

Bihr, A. and Pfefferkorn, R. (2002) *Hommes, femmes, quelle égalité?* Paris: Éditions de l'Atelier and Éditions Ouvrières, pp. 130–131.

Bohannan, P. (1967) *African Homicide and Suicide*. New York: Atheneum.

Boltanski, L. (1971) 'Les usages sociaux du corps', *Les Annales ESC* 1: 205–233.

Bonnemère, P. (1992) 'Suicide et homicide: deux modalités vindicatoires en Nouvelle-Guinée', *Stanford French Review* 16: 19–43.

Bosma, H., Peter, R., Siegrist, J. and Marmot, M. (1998), 'Two alternative job stress models and the risk of coronary heart disease', *American Journal of Public Health* 88: 68–74.

Bourgoin, N. (1997) 'Le suicide dans la Police nationale', *Population* 52 (2): 429–440.

—— (1999) 'Suicide et activité professionnelle', *Population* 54 (1): 73–102.

Canguilhem, G. (1966) *On the Normal and the Pathological*, trans. C.R. Fawcett, in collaboration with R.S. Cohen. New York: Zone Books, 1991.

Castel, R. (1995) *Les Métamorphoses de la question sociale*, Paris: Fayard.

Chauvel, L. (1997) 'L'uniformisation du taux de suicide masculin selon l'âge: effet de génération, ou recomposition du cycle de vie?' *Revue française de sociologie* XXXVIII, 4: 681–733.

Chenu, A. (1990) *L'Archipel des employés*, collection *Études*. Paris: INSEE.

Chesnais, J.-C. (1973) 'L'évolution de la mortalité par suicide dans différents pays industrialisés', *Population* 2: 419–422.

—— (1981) *Histoire de la violence*. Paris: Robert Laffont.

Counts, D.A. (1984), 'Revenge suicide by Lusi women', in D. O'Brien and S.W. Tiffany, eds, *Rethinking Women's Roles*. Berkeley: University of California Press, pp. 71–83.

Cutler, D.M., Glaeser, E.L. and Norberg, K.E. (2004) 'Explaining the rise in youth suicide', NBER, *Working Paper* no. 7713.

Degenne, A. and Forsé, M. (1994) *Les Réseaux sociaux*. Paris: Armand Colin.

Desplanques, G. (1993) 'L'inégalité sociale devant la mort', *Données sociales: la société française*. Paris: INSEE.

Devereux, G. (1951) *Reality and Dream: The Psychotherapy of a Plains Indian*. New York: International Universities Press.

Douglas, J. (1967) *The Social Meanings of Suicide*. Princeton, New Jersey: Princeton University Press.

Drever, F. and Bunting, J. (1996) 'Patterns and trends in male mortality' in F. Drever and M. Whitehead, eds, *Health Inequalities*. London: Office for National Statistics.

Dublin, L. and Bunzel, B. (1933) *To Be or Not to Be: a Study of Suicide*. New York: Harrison Smith & Robert Haas.

Dubois, Abbé J.A. (1985) *Mœurs, institutions et cérémonies des peuples de l'Inde*. Pondichéry: Alliance française and Paris: A.-M. Métaillié.

Duchac, R. (1964) 'Suicide au Japon, suicide à la japonaise', *Revue française de sociologie* V: 402–415.

Durkheim, É. (1895) *The Rules of Sociological Method and Selected Texts on Sociology and its Method*, ed. and intro. by S. Lukes; trans. W.D. Halls. London: Macmillan, 1982.

—— (1897) *On Suicide*, trans. R. Buss. London: Penguin, 2006.

—— (1898) 'Individualism and the intellectuals', trans. M. Traugott in R.N. Bellah, ed., *Émile Durkheim on Morality and Society*. Chicago: University of Chicago Press, 1973, pp. 42–57.

Elias, N. (1939) *The Civilizing Process*, trans. E. Jephcott. Oxford: Basil Blackwell, 1978 and 1982.

—— (1982) *The Society of Individuals*, trans. E. Jephcott. Oxford: Basil Blackwell, 1991.

Elisseeff, D. (2001) *La Femme au temps des empereurs de Chine*. Paris: Payot, pp. 57–58.

Fassin, D. (2000) 'Qualifier les inégalités' in A. Leclerc, D. Fassin *et al.*, eds, *Les Inégalités sociales de santé*. Paris: La Découverte and INSERM.

Fourastié, J. (1979) *Les Trente Glorieuses, ou La Révolution invisible de 1946 à 1975*. Paris: Fayard.

Freeman, L.C. and Thomson, C.R. (1989) 'Estimating acquaintanceship' in M. Koshen, ed., *The Small World*. Norwood, New Jersey: Ablex Publishing, pp. 147–158.

Freudenberger, H.J. (1980) *Burnout: How to Beat the High Cost of Success*. New York: Bantam Press.

Garbe, C. (1993) 'Les femmes et la lecture', in *Identité, lecture, écriture*, collection *Études et recherches*. Paris: Bibliothèque publique d'information/ Centre Pompidou.

Gini, C. (1931) 'Intorno alle curve di concentrazione', *Bulletin de l'Institut international de la statistique* XXVI: 423–475.

Girard, A., Bastide, H., Clerc, P. and Sauvy, A. (1970) *Population et l'enseignement*. Paris: PUF.

Goffman, E. (1967) *Interaction: Essays on Face-to-Face Behaviour*. Garden City, New York: Anchor Books.

Granovetter, M. (1973) 'The strength of weak ties', *American Journal of Sociology* 78 (8): 1360–1380.

Guillaumat-Taillet, F., Malpot, J.J. and Paquel, V. (1996) *Le patrimoine des ménages: répartition et concentration*. *Données sociales*, Paris: INSEE, pp. 345–361.

Guillemard, A.-M. (1972) *La Retraite, une mort sociale*. Paris: PUF.

Halbwachs, M. (1930) *The Causes of Suicide*, trans. H. Goldblatt. London: Routledge & Kegan Paul, 1978.

Halliburton, M. (1998) 'Suicide: a paradox of development in Kerala', *Economic and Political Weekly* 33: 36–37.

Hamermesh, D.S. and Soss, N.M. (1974) 'An economic theory of suicide', *Journal of Political Economy* (University of Chicago Press) 82 (1): 83–98.

Hanus, M. (2004) *Le Deuil après suicide*. Paris: Maloine.

Hassan, R. (1983) *A Way of Dying: Suicide in Singapore*. Kuala Lumpur: Oxford University Press.

Helliwell, J.F. (2004) 'Well-being and social capital: does suicide pose a puzzle?' National Bureau of Economic Research, *Working Paper* no. 10896, November.

Héran, F. (1988a) 'Un monde sélectif: les associations', *Économie et statistique* no. 208, March.

Héran, F. (1988b) 'La sociabilité, une pratique culturelle', *Économie et statistique* no. 216, December.

Hilico, C. and Didier, P. (2004) 'Les départements métropolitains: similitudes et oppositions socio-économiques', *INSEE Première* no. 943, January.

Inglehart, R. (2000) 'Globalization and postmodern values', *The Washington Quarterly*, winter, pp. 215–228.

—— and Baker, W.E. (2000) 'Modernization, cultural change and the persistence of traditional values', *American Sociological Review* 65: 19–51.

Jonas, H. (1979) *The Imperative of Responsibility: In Search of Ethics for the Technological Age.* University of Chicago Press.

Jougla, É. *et al.* (2000) 'La mortalité' in A. Leclerc, D. Fassin *et al.*, eds, *Les Inégalités sociales de santé.* Paris: La Découverte and INSERM.

——, Pequignot, F., Chappert, J.-L., Rossolin, F., Le Toullec, A. and Pavillon, G. (2002) 'La qualité des données de mortalité sur le suicide', *Revue d'épidémiologie et de santé publique* 50: 49–62.

Kelly, S. and Bunting, J. (1998) 'Trend in suicide in England and Wales 1982–1996', *Statistical News* no. 119, spring. London.

Kessler, D., Masson, A. and Strauss-Kahn, D. (1982) *Accumulation et répartition des patrimoines. Colloque internationale du CNRS 1978, Préface d'André Babeau.* Paris: Economica and Éditions du CNRS.

Kumar, K.A. (1995) 'Suicide in Kerala from a mental health perspective' in G. Joseph *et al.*, eds, *Suicide in Perspective: With Special Reference to Kerala.* Rajagiri: CHCRE-HAFA.

La Fontaine, J. (1967) 'Homicide and suicide among the Gisu' in P. Bohannan, ed., *African Homicide and Suicide.* New York: Atheneum.

Lanciano, C., Maurice, M., Silvestre, J.-J. and Nohara, N., eds (1998) *Les Acteurs de l'innovation et l'Entreprise: France–Europe–Japon.* Paris: L'Harmattan.

Lang, T. and Ribet, C. (2000) 'Les maladies cardio-vasculaires' in A. Leclerc, D. Fassin *et al.*, eds, *Les Inégalités sociales de santé.* Paris: La Découverte and INSERM.

Ledina, N.B. (1999) *La Vie quotidienne d'une ville soviétique. Saint-Pétersbourg entre 1920 et 1930.* Saint Petersburg: Letnii Sad.

Lee, S. and Kleiman, A. (2000) 'Suicide as resistance in Chinese society' in E.J. Perry and M. Selden, eds, *Chinese Society, Change, Conflict and Resistance.* London: Routledge, pp. 221–240.

Lollivier, S. and Verger, D. (1990) 'Le patrimoine aujourd'hui: beaucoup entre les mains de quelques-uns', *Données sociales 1990.* Paris: INSEE, pp. 167–174.

Lombrail, P. (2000) 'Accès aux soins' in A. Leclerc, D. Fassin *et al.*, eds, *Les Inégalités de santé.* Paris: La Découverte and INSERM.

MacDonald, C.J.H. (2003) 'An anthropological investigation of suicide in Palawan, Philippines', *South East Asian Studies* 4 (4): 419–435.

Maddison, A. (2001), *L'Économie mondiale: statistiques mondiales.* Paris: OCDE.

—— (2005) *L'Économie mondiale: une perspective millénaire*. Paris: OCDE.

Malinowski, B. (1926) *Crime and Custom in Savage Society*. London: Routledge & Kegan Paul, new edn 1966.

Mannheim, K. (1928) 'The problem of generations' in *Essays on the Sociology of Knowledge*. London: Routledge & Kegan Paul, 1952.

Maris, R.W. (1969) *Social Forces in Urban Suicide*. Homewood, Illinois: The Dorsey Press.

Maurice, M. and Nohara, H., eds (1999) *Les Mutations du 'modèle' japonais de l'entreprise*. Paris: La Documentation française, series *Problèmes politiques et sociaux* no. 820, March.

Mayer, P. and Ziaian, T. (2002) 'Indian suicide and marriage: a research note', *Journal of Comparative Family Studies* XXXIII (2): 297–305.

Mead, G.H. (1934) *Mind, Self and Society: From the Standpoint of a Social Behaviourist*. Chicago: University of Chicago Press.

Mendras, H. (1962) *La fin des paysans*. Paris: SEDEIS, new edn Babel 1991.

Merveilles de l'Europe (1963) collection *Réalités*. Paris: Hachette, p. 174.

Meslé, F., Shkolnikov, V.M., Hertrich, V. and Vallin, J. (1992, 1996) *La Crise sanitaire dans les pays de l'ex-URSS: Tendances récentes de la mortalité par cause en Russie, Données statistiques 1965–1994*. Paris: INED and Moscow Centre for Demography and Human Ecology, 2 vols.

Mesrine, A. (1999) 'Les différences de mortalité par milieu social restent fortes', *Données sociales*. Paris: La Documentation française and INSEE.

Morishima, M. (1987) *Le Capitalisme et le Confucianisme*. Paris: Flammarion.

Pan Ké Shon, J.-L. (2003) 'Isolement relationnel et mal-être'. *INSEE Première* no.931, November.

Panzac, D. (2003) *Le Docteur Adrien Proust, père méconnu, précurseur oublié*. Paris: L'Harmattan, pp. 90–91.

Parthasarathy, G. (1998) 'Suicide of cotton farmers in Andhra Pradesh: an exploratory study', *Economic and Political Weekly* 33 (13): 720–726.

Paugam, S. (2005) *Les Formes élémentaires de la pauvreté*. Paris: PUF.

Perrot, M. ed. (1987) *Histoire de la vie privée*, vol. IV: *De la Révolution à la Grande Guerre*. Paris: Seuil.

Phillips, M.R., Li, X. and Zhang, Y. (2002) 'Suicide rates in China 1995–99', *The Lancet* 359 (9): 835–840.

Piketty, T. (2001) *Les Hauts Revenus en France au XXe siècle. Inégalités et redistributions, 1901–1998*. Paris: Grasset.

Pinguet, M. (1984) *Voluntary Death in Japan*, trans. R. Morris. Cambridge: Polity, 1993.

Pinnow, K.M. (2000) 'Cutting and counting: forensic medicine as a science of society in Bolshevik Russia 1920–29' in D.L. Hoffmann and Y. Kotsonis, eds, *Russian Modernity: Politics, Knowledge and Practice*. New York: Macmillan Press and St Martin's Press.

PNUD [UNDP] (1995) 'Comment mesurer l'inégalité sociologique entre les sexes?' *Rapport mondial sur le développement humain*, ch. III. Paris: Economica, pp. 77–92.

Powell, E.H. (1958) 'Occupation, status and suicide: towards a redefinition of anomie', *American Sociological Review* vol. 23, April.

Prassad, C.D. (1999) 'Suicide deaths and quality of Indian cotton: perspectives from history of technology and Khadi movement', *Economic and Political Weekly* 24 (5): 12.

Prost, A., ed. (1987) *Histoire de la vie privée*, vol. V: *De la Première Guerre mondiale à nos jours*. Paris: Seuil.

Rittersporn, G.T. (1997) 'Le message des données introuvables: l'État et les statistiques du suicide en Russie et en URSS', *Cahiers du monde russe* 4: 511–523.

Ruzicka, L.T. (1996) 'A note on suicide in Russia 1965–1993', *Journal of the Australian Population Association*, vol. 13, no. 2, November.

Savorgnan, F. (1930) 'Di alcuni metodi per misurare la distribuzione des redditi in Austria (1903–1910). Communication au Congrès internationale de statistique de Tokyo 1930', *Bulletin de l'Institut international de la statistique* XXV: 331–353.

Schnapper, D. (1991) *L'Épreuve du chômage*. Paris: Gallimard, new edn 1994.

Schumpeter, J. (1942) *Capitalism, Socialism and Democracy*. London: Allen and Unwin.

Sen, A. (1992) *Inequality Reexamined*. Oxford: Clarendon Press.

Shelly, M. (2002) Epidemiological study by the AREMEDIA Association and INSERM. *British Medical Journal*, July.

Sola Pool, I. de (1978) 'Contacts and influence', *Social Networks* 1: 147–154.

Suicides en URSS 1922–1925 (1927) *URSS Statistique* vol. XXXV, part 1. Moscow: Section de la statistique morale, p. 14.

Surault, P. (1991) 'Post-modernité et inégalités sociales devant la mort', *Cahiers de sociologie et de démographie médicales* 2: 121–143.

—— (1995a) 'Variations sur les variations du suicide en France', *Population* 4–5: 983–1012.

—— (1995b) 'Inégalités sociales devant la santé et la vie dans les pays du Nord' in H. Gérard and V. Piché, eds, *Sociologie des populations*. Montréal: PUM/AUPELF-UREF, pp. 235–255.

—— (1997) 'Suicide et milieu social: éléments d'analyse' in J.-J. Chavagnat and R. Franc, eds, *Suicide et vie professionelle: les risques du métier. XXVIIIe Journées du Groupement d'études et prévention du suicide*. Toulouse: STARSUP Éditions, March–April, pp. 57–82.

—— (2003) 'Approche socio-démographique de la santé mentale', *Actes de la journée de restitution régionale ARPCIMEP-ORSPEC*. Poitiers, 1 October, p. 64.

Tartarin, R. (2004) 'Transfusion sanguine et immortalité chez Alexandr Bogdanov' in A. Supiot, ed., *Tisser le lien social*. Nantes: Éditions de la MSH.

Townsend, P. (1970) *The Concept of Poverty*. London: Heinemann.

Vallet, L.-A. and Caille. J.-P. (1996) 'Les élèves étrangers ou issus de l'immigration dans l'école et le collège français: une étude d'ensemble, *Éducation et formations* no. 67, April.

Vandermeersch, L. (2002) 'Le suicide en Chine' in G. Morel *et al.*, eds, *Clinique du suicide*. Ramonville: Éditions Érès, pp. 53–56.

Vincent, S. (2001) *Le Jouet et ses usages sociaux*. Paris: La Dispute and SNEDIT.

WHO (1997) *Rapport mondial sur le développement humain*. Geneva: WHO.

—— (1999) *Figures and Facts about Suicide*. Geneva: WHO.

Index